Absolute Beginner's Guide to Networking

Second Edition

Mark Gibbs
Contributing Author: Todd Brown

SAMS
PUBLISHING

201 West 103rd Street
Indianapolis, Indiana 46290

For my son, Keihan.

Copyright © 1995 by Sams Publishing

SECOND EDITION

International Standard Book Number: 0-672-30553-4

Library of Congress Catalog Card Number: 94-67081

98   97   96   95   4   3   2

Interpretation of the printing code: the rightmost double-digit number is the year of the book's printing; the rightmost single-digit, the number of the book's printing. For example, a printing code of 95-1 shows that the first printing of the book occurred in 1995.

Composed in AGaramond and MCPdigital by Macmillan Computer Publishing

Printed in the United States of America

Trademarks

Publisher
Richard K. Swadley

Acquisitions Manager
Greg Wiegand

Managing Editor
Cindy Morrow

Acquisitions Editor
Rosemarie Graham

Development Editor
Angelique Brittingham

Production Editor
Sean Medlock

Copy Editor
Ryan Rader

Editorial Coordinator
Bill Whitmer

Editorial Assistants
Carol Ackerman
Sharon Cox
Lynette Quinn

Technical Reviewers
Todd Brown
Robert Smith

Marketing Manager
Gregg Bushyeager

Cover Designer
Tim Amrhein

Book Designer
Alyssa Yesh

**Director of Production
and Manufacturing**
Jeff Valler

Imprint Manager
Juli Cook

**Manufacturing
Coordinator**
Paul Gilchrist

Production Analysts
Dennis Hager
Mary Beth Wakefield

**Graphics Image
Specialists**
Tim Montgomery
Dennis Sheehan
Susan VandeWalle

Production
Georgina Briggs
Elaine Brush
Cheryl Cameron
Charlotte Clapp
Mary Ann Cosby
Stephen Carlin
DiMonique Ford
David Garratt
Kimberly K. Hannel
Donna Harbin
Aleata Howard
Ayanna Lacey
Malinda Lowder
Shawn MacDonald
Erika Millen
Wendy Ott
Chad Poore
Casey Price
Brian-Kent Proffitt
Scott Tullis
SA Springer
A. Wimmer
Holly Wittenberg

Indexer
Greg Eldred

Overview

Contents

Foreword

In one of my favorite Sunday-afternoon slouchfest movies, Lulu asks the lyrical question, "How do you thank someone who has taken you from crayons to perfume?"

To which I add, "How do thank someone who's given you the perfect squeegee, dead whales, Bill: The Little Red Hen, and the seven deadly sins of networking?"

If you're Sidney Pointier in "To Sir With Love," your thanks is another year teaching in a seedy London school.

If you're Mark Gibbs, you're rewarded with a lucrative columnist contract with *Network World* and universal adulation from our readers.

Well, sort of.

Mark thinks the contract could be more lucrative, and our readers don't always love what Mark has to say. His insights into networking leave readers laughing and sometimes downright angry.

And that's a good thing. Because whatever their reaction, Mark makes people think about networking: what it can do for their companies and their profit margins.

Intelligent use of network technologies can help your company, large or small, provide better service and better products to customers. But too often companies get sidetracked in their network efforts by things that have little to do with technology.

Gibbs' gift lies in exploring the oft-ignored issues that determine whether a company will be successful in deploying technology or will fail. He looks at the product zealotry, the management foibles, the outdated thinking, and the petty politics that foil even the best-laid plans.

He uses satire, sarcasm, and dry British humor to help people see things more clearly. His artful analogies to squeegees and Little Red Hens open readers' eyes. (You gotta read these columns.) Sometimes they like what they see, sometimes they don't.

But Mark also does a heck of a job helping people understand networking, which is considered only slightly less arcane a subject than particle physics.

He has a knack for boiling down the most complicated network topics to simple concepts that help even seasoned information systems pros get a better grasp of things. That's why he's the best author for the job ahead. This book is designed to usher you into the world of networking, and you couldn't ask for a better guide.

So sit back and enjoy the ride. You'll come to love networking just like Mark and me. At the very least, you'll learn enough to hold your own in any conversation about nodes and baud rates and NOSes.

Just keep your eyes peeled for the dead whales.

John Gallant

Editor-in-Chief, *Network World*

Acknowledgments

I must start by thanking my gorgeous wife, Arianne, who has been unfailingly wonderful, encouraging, and supportive, and my son, Keihan, the most perfect child in the world, who adds no end of motivation to the creative process. (The thought of college fees focuses the mind wonderfully.)

At Sams, thank you to Rosemarie Graham, who was a great resource in the first edition and made me write the second edition. Thanks also to everyone else at Sams who worked on this project.

I would also like to thank Debra Young at CompuServe for her support.

The following are various products and services that made the creation of this tome so much easier and even, at times, more fun:

✖ CompuServe and the CompuServe Information Manager for Windows (WinCIM) from CompuServe, Inc. WinCIM provides an interface for accessing CompuServe that's a real pleasure to use, and CompuServe itself is immeasurably useful.

✖ Designer and Picture Publisher from Micrografx, Inc. Designer was used for almost all of the figures in this book. It's robust, fast, and reliable—a rare combination. Picture Publisher was used to mess with a few of the screen shots and to edit some bitmap images used in figures.

✖ Microsoft Corporation's Excel for Windows. Used for all sorts of tables.

✖ Word for Windows—the world's best word processor. Used for hacking out words.

✖ KTWV, The Wave, the finest radio station in Los Angeles. It made for great listening during those 2 a.m. sessions.

✖ Lipton Tea (the brisk one), which kept me going. Through both editions.

✖ Quotes On Line, AskSam Systems. Used to augment my collection of quotes—if you're a fan of quotations, buy this. You'll love it.

✖ Visio, Shapeware Corporation. Used for the flowcharts.

About the Authors

For more than a decade, Mark Gibbs has consulted, lectured, developed technical and service operations, and written articles and books about the network market. Mark was a co-founder of Novell's UK operation, where he was responsible for the management of all technical services. He was with Novell for five years, and since leaving has pursued a successful career as an independent consultant and analyst. He has written books on networking for Macmillan (*Navigating the Internet, Do It Yourself Networking with LANtastic,* and *Networking Personal Computers*), and has contributed articles about PCs and networking technology to various journals and periodicals. He is also a contributing editor and columnist for the industry weekly *Network World.*

Mark can be contacted at Gibbs & Co., (805) 647-2307, through CompuServe, [71333,3716], or on the Internet, mgibbs@rain.org.

Todd Brown is from the Muncie, Indiana area. He attended Wes-Del High School in Gaston, Indiana, and Ball State University in Muncie.

Todd began his work in the microcomputer industry in 1986 as a Sales Representative for ComputerLand. He quickly became interested in networking, and took his first formal NetWare training course in 1987. Since that time, Todd has become certified as a Novell ECNE (Enterprise Certified NetWare Engineer). His other certifications include OS/2, Windows, and the maintenance and optimization of IBM, Compaq, and Apple Macintosh hardware platforms.

Todd has worked in the Indianapolis area for the past 5 years as a Systems Engineer at LMB Microcomputers. He enjoys his work in the microcomputer industry, and hopes that you can enjoy it along with him through his work here. He revised Chapter 8 and Appendix C, as well as writing Chapter 14.

Introduction

Networking can't be avoided. From its humble beginnings as a way of making expensive peripherals cost-effective to its current information-systems superstar status (beat that, Robin Leach), networking has become an accepted part of business computer technology. But that doesn't mean networking is simple. It's a complex subject, and this book is here to lead you through the network jungle.

This book gives you the information you need to know before you get too involved with the user's manuals for your network. It's a guide to the history, technology, and usage of local area networks. Complex topics are covered in simple terms, and the key features of the major networking products (both the operating systems and the applications) are described so that you can understand how and where they fit into the network picture.

By the end of this book, you'll no longer be phased by questions like, "What kind of NOS does your server run?" You'll find out why peer-to-peer networking is becoming popular. At dinner parties, you'll be able to expound eloquently on the technology of NetWare's System Fault Tolerance and parry questions on the merits of EtherNet over ARCnet. You'll also find that this book whitens your clothes and removes those stubborn stains.

In short, if you want to find out what networking is all about but were too afraid to ask (or fell asleep during the answer), this book was written for you.

Who Should Read This Book?

The title of this book says it all. If you have just discovered that a network is going to affect your work life, want to find out what this newfangled technology is all about, or are trying to find out if a network would help your organization, this book is for you. The *Absolute Beginner's Guide to Networking* is aimed at three different groups of people:

- ✖ Individuals who know nothing about networking, but who want to find out what it's all about.
- ✖ Companies that want to find out how networking can help their business.
- ✖ Schools that need a basis for introductory computer networking classes.

Conventions Used in This Book

The following typographic conventions are used in this book:

- ✖ Code lines, variables, and any text you see onscreen appear in `monospace` font.
- ✖ New terms appear in *italics*.

Each chapter begins with a list of questions. These questions are designed to prepare you for the important points you'll encounter in the chapter.

Within each chapter you'll encounter several icons that indicate the direction of the current topic. Their meaning should be clear when you see them used in the context of the book. The next few paragraphs explain each icon and its associated text.

NOTE:

A Note brings a particular topic to your attention when further thought is warranted. It often describes what others might do in a given situation.

Clue: A Clue is an insight into a certain topic. It often appears just after a subject is explained, and provides a more detailed explanation of what's going on. If you skip a Clue you'll still be able to understand the material, but you won't have the extra insight that the Clue provides.

PITFALL:

A Pitfall focuses your attention on a problem or side effect that can occur in a specific situation. It often attempts to steer you away from a course of action that gives others trouble.

WARNING:

A Warning is more forceful than a Pitfall. When you see a Warning, read it carefully—it will help you avoid possible problems.

> **REWARD:**
>
> A Reward shows you an extra shortcut or advantage that's possible with the command or subject you just learned. It's a tip that will help you streamline your approach to the material being discussed.

The Path to Networking

Your path to understanding networks starts with the acceptance of the fact that although computer technology is complex, full of acronyms (PC, DOS, LAN, MIPS, MHz, and so on) and buzzwords (spooler, ping, roll back, interrupt, and so on), and often seems to be completely antithetical to the maintenance of a calm and balanced outlook on life, it also has an important place in doing business and running our lives. Moreover, computer networking is becoming one of the most important areas of computing. It has graduated from expensive and exotic to reasonably priced and prosaic. Like the other books in this series, The *Absolute Beginner's Guide to Networking* promises you excitement and adventure. You'll seek out new technologies and products. You'll boldly go into the future. You might even find a job there.

The History of PCs and Networking

1

1. How long have PCs been around?

2. How long did dinosaurs rule the earth?

3. What was the name of the first electromechanical computer?

4. How many computers did Howard Aiken predict the world would need?

5. What was batch computing?

6. Why didn't people stick with using mainframes?

7. Why did minicomputers become popular?

8. Why did PCs become popular?

9. What is a network?

10. What was a disk server and why was it inadequate as a network server solution?

It's hard to believe that the history of personal computers (PCs) and networking is only 13 years old. In that time, PCs have evolved from expensive novelties to fundamental business tools. ("Yes son, there was a time when Daddy used a typewriter and no one had ever played Flight Simulator…")

Businesses have moved from reliance on the traditional business computing tools (mainframes and minicomputers) to microcomputer-based systems—a trend called *rightsizing*.

More than any other PC technology, networking—the set of techniques for connecting computers so that they can share resources and information—has made this transition possible.

Networking, as you will see, has changed forever the way computers are used. This chapter looks at the history of computers, the evolutionary forces of the marketplace that made PCs so important, and the critical role of networks in business.

When Mainframes Ruled the Earth

The story of mainframes and minicomputers and their success and decline is reminiscent of the history of dinosaurs. Over a long period and at a relatively leisurely pace, dinosaurs evolved. They went from simple creatures that hauled themselves out of the sea, took a gasp of air, and decided that the land looked more interesting than the water to the dominant life form that ruled the earth for approximately 150 million years (give or take a century).

Just as they were settling down for another millennium of dominance, something happened (no one is quite sure what), and the latest evolutionary trend—mammals—rushed in to take their place. The story of the computing world could cast the mainframes and minicomputers as the dinosaurs and the PCs as the mammals. Unlike the dinosaurs, however, the mainframes haven't become extinct, although they no longer rule.

Out of the Sea

Just to give you a bit of background, the first electronic (actually, electromechanical) computer was ENIAC—rated as one of the most important inventions of the Second World War. (The other, of course, was the atomic bomb.) ENIAC stood for Electronic Numerical Integrator, Analyzer, and Computer.

ENIAC had a mean time between failures (that is, the time that it could run without fouling up somehow) of about 30 seconds, and it took all sorts of tricks to make it productive. Unless you wanted to take a census, calculate ballistics trajectories, or something similar, ENIAC was of limited use in business. To those who used it (mainly the U.S. military, to produce tables of artillery calculations), it was invaluable. It logged more than 80,000 hours of calculation until it was finally switched off on October 2, 1955.

A series of other electronic computers of increasing power and sophistication followed, leading to the introduction in 1953 of the IBM 701, the world's first commercial programmable electronic computer. (One of the early computing pioneers, Howard Aiken, projected that no more than six electronic computers would ever be sold commercially.)

Tyranocomputerus Mainframus

During the period from the mid-fifties through the sixties, computing was very expensive. I'm not just talking a little pricey here. In the beginning it was a case of "Oh, good heavens, automation seemed like a good idea until I saw the price tag, but I guess using people is cheaper."

The first era in the commercial use of computers was based on batch computing, the first way of making the best use of limited and expensive resources and the first effective way of torturing both users and programmers. Batch computing was based on program instructions submitted on cards or punched paper tape.

> **NOTE:**
> As a historical footnote, punched cards were invented by a statistician named Herman Hollerith. The U.S. government was in danger of drowning in the paperwork with the 1890 census, and Hollerith invented the punched card system to store the data. The company that Hollerith formed to exploit his idea eventually became the International Business Machines Corporation.

The patterns of holes on the card or tape were read by the machine and translated into instructions or data and acted upon. A set of cards or tapes was called a *job*, and dropping a deck of cards for a large program (400 or 500 cards, for example) was one of the most infuriating fumbles possible.

Because many people wanted the computer to run their programs and the computer could only do so much work, the jobs were *batched*, and the machines were usually run around the clock.

This method was frustrating for users and programmers because they had to wait to see if their jobs worked. (Sometimes the wait was as much as 24 hours.) If a user made one error, perhaps leaving out one card, using a wrong instruction, or mispunching a card or the tape, the job would fail—back to the drawing board to correct the error and try again! Needless to say, this process could go on for a long time with large programs.

Another problem with this method was that mainframes were (and still are) expensive. They were expensive to own (for many mainframes, you could only lease them) and house. They were physically big, required air conditioning and their own main power, and were delicate. They require skilled keepers and managers as well as teams of skilled technicians (the priests and acolytes of the mainframe systems) to keep them running.

This unfortunately meant that unless your job was important in corporate terms, you were on the standby list. Until machine time was available, you had to wait. If you needed software developed to do a particular job that wasn't a corporate priority, you had to wait. Programmers were scarce and their time expensive.

Today, user friendliness in computer systems is an important issue. Users expect software to be fast and easy to use. In the mainframe systems, however, user friendliness was irrelevant. Their job was computation and tabulation, and, for the low-priority user, this often resulted in exasperation.

Mainframes ushered in the first era of automation, and corporations developed a love affair with the mainframe. Where a repetitive task was involved, particularly in areas such as accounting or stock control, the mainframe was a better deal than people. It was not only more cost-effective in terms of work produced per dollar, but it was also more accurate, could work around the clock, and didn't need coffee breaks or holidays.

This established the Data Processing department. DP, as it became called, did exactly what its name implied—it processed data. Data (such as orders and hours worked) was fed in, and processed data (such as invoices and paychecks) was output.

The great mainframe dinosaurs, digitally speaking, owned the corporation. The Itty Bitty Machine Corporation (a.k.a. IBM) became the dominant market force in computing, and the mainframe was the "true" way for the Data Processing zealots. (See Figure 1.1.)

New Bits on the Block

In the sixties, a heretical new type of computer appeared: the minicomputer. These machines were cheaper, physically smaller, didn't need air conditioning, and were to a great extent easier to use (at least by the standards of the day). The priests of the mainframes shuddered.

Figure 1.1.
An IBM mainframe, circa 1958.

Although owning a mainframe was a corporate issue because of the expense involved, a department could own a minicomputer because they didn't need to make special provisions for housing and they didn't need to have the level of expertise required to run a mainframe. In short, minicomputers were affordable.

This development also introduced a new character to the computer scene. The minicomputer replaced the clean-cut mainframe types with a new breed of programmer. Because minicomputers were cheaper, they started to appear in universities and other educational institutions. And because they were more accessible and designed for modification and extension, they attracted a group of enthusiasts who became known as hackers.

These hackers, however, were not of the same breed as the notorious variety of today. These hackers were people filled with enthusiasm for computing, people who wanted to make better, "neater," and more efficient software. From their ranks rose some of the people who would shape the personal computer revolution.

The minicomputer market grew rapidly. When departments could justify them, minicomputers were installed. This was the environment that made the Digital Equipment Corporation (DEC) the second largest computer company in the world. (See Figure 1.2.)

Figure 1.2.
A DEC PDP-8, one of the first minicomputers, which led Digital Equipment Corporation to become the second largest computer manufacturer in the world.

As the software improved, the range of functions that could be automated increased. A minicomputer could support several users simultaneously, a process called time-sharing. Each user could view the system as if it belonged to him or her alone, and could run programs, manipulate data, and even create software. Mainframe technology also made a degree of adaptation to this market. Sophisticated time-sharing systems and increasingly powerful hardware and software products were developed pretty much in tandem with the minicomputer market.

This, then, was the computer scene during the late seventies: mainframes and minicomputers fulfilled corporate and primarily departmental roles, respectively. For the tasks they could do and the way they could do them, they were good. They brought new, more efficient practices to the office and made business more productive. They failed, however, in the area of personal productivity (making workers, rather than the corporation, more efficient).

The Rise of the Personal Computer

In the mid-seventies, a new technology appeared: the microprocessor. These devices used many connected transistors to make a computing device that fit onto a chip of silicon.

The first microprocessors were, by today's standards, pretty simple. The very first microprocessor, a 4-bit design that became known as the 4004, was designed by an Intel engineer, Marcian E. "Ted" Hoff, in 1969. Intel's client was a Japanese company that went bankrupt in 1970, and Intel couldn't decide whether or not to put the chip on the market. They did, and by 1974 there were more than 19 microprocessors on the market, including the one that became the springboard for today's PC industry—the Intel 8088.

Microprocessors were initially targeted as controllers—devices for managing the operation of dishwashers and refrigerators. But the potential of these devices as real computers wasn't missed by the manufacturers, computer system designers, and enthusiasts. (See Figure 1.3.)

The 8080, the Z-80, and CP/M

Among the first microprocessor market successes was the Intel 8080, and a new operating system called CP/M-80 was written to support this chip. CP/M-80 was created in 1975 by Gary Kildall, the founder and president of Digital Research, Incorporated, which was arguably the first vendor of a real microcomputer operating system. The company has now become a division of Novell Incorporated, the biggest market force in networking operating systems today.

CP/M stood for Control Program/Microcomputers—a snappy product name if ever there was one.

Figure 1.3.
The Intel 8080 and Zilog Z-80 microprocessor.

> **NOTE:**
>
> The term *operating system* is one you've probably heard many times. The operating system is a program that manages and controls other programs' access to the resources of the computer. If you think of a computer in terms of a car, the operating system is like the car's control systems (accelerator, brake, clutch, speedometer, RPM gauge, fuel gauge, and so on). The application program is the equivalent of the driver, and the hardware components are like the engine, transmission, and so on. The user's interface to the system is like the controls, both those that enable you to change speed, change gears, and so on, and those that tell you about the status of the car (fuel gauge, oil pressure gauge). (I'll talk more about this subject later.)

This operating system was, in its time, "hot." If you had an 8080 or Z-80 system running CP/M, with a pair of 8" floppy drives and 64 kilobytes of RAM, you had a state-of-the-art system that would make other enthusiasts green with envy. To go beyond this and earn their hatred, all you needed was a hard disk and a printer, both of which were serious expenditures.

Hard disks at this time were particularly interesting. The first ones widely used with microcomputer-based systems had 14" drives (compare that with today's 3.25" hard disk drives) and access times that seemed as long as coffee breaks.

Along with CP/M eventually came a whole collection of applications, development languages, and tools. Many of today's hardware and software vendors and PC dealers owe their rise and success to the CP/M market.

Apple Bites

In 1976, Apple Computer, a company now well-known for having been started in a garage, was getting off the ground. Founded by the now-legendary Steve Jobs and Steve Wozniak, Apple is credited with establishing the roots of the PC industry. Although the story of Visicalc and the Apple II computer is well known, it's worth covering once more because it illustrates the key to the PC revolution.

In the mid-seventies, if you wanted to play "what if" games with calculations on a mainframe, you had to write a program, debug it, try some data, check the results, try some more data, and so on. It was a pretty laborious process, and not really practical unless what you were doing was of corporate importance and you had plenty of time. This situation motivated two students from the Harvard Business School to develop the world's first useful microcomputer spreadsheet: Visicalc.

The Apple II was based on the Motorola 6502 processor (an 8-bit design), could have up to 128 kilobytes of RAM, and used a tape cassette drive for program and data storage. *8-bit* describes the size of the data that the processor can handle. Apple struck a deal with the creators of Visicalc that made the program exclusively available on the Apple II. This program is credited with catapulting Apple from revenues of $800,000 in 1977 to just under $48 million in 1979.

Business users bought the Apple II just to run Visicalc, and in Visicalc's wake came a whole raft of applications that gave users dedicated, easily accessed computer power for the first time at a reasonable price.

IBM Takes Over

The computers I've been talking about, the CP/M machines and the Apples, weren't called personal computers when they were introduced—this wasn't a recognized term until August 1981, the birthdate of the IBM PC. But it was the market created by those microcomputer systems that made the IBM PC possible.

Although the IBM PC was launched in 1981, the microprocessor it was built on was introduced in 1974. The Intel 8088 was a 16-bit microprocessor that could access larger memory and run much faster than its predecessors. IBM commissioned a little-known company called Microsoft to develop an operating system. The rest, as they say, is history.

The IBM PC went on to define a standard, or more properly, a series of standards that has resulted in the sale of roughly 100 million PCs since 1981. (See Figure 1.4.) What made the IBM PC such a success was IBM's marketing muscle. IBM had the money and the market presence to make the IBM Personal Computer acceptable in big corporations. Although it's easy to criticize IBM for the many mistakes it made in developing the PC market and its lack of responsiveness to a market that grew faster than it could handle, without IBM's involvement, the market would have grown more slowly and in a more fragmented way.

Figure 1.4.
The IBM Personal Computer, which defined a standard and an industry, was launched in August of 1981.

The IBM PC continued the trend that the Apple II had started: it made computing power available to business users. The opportunity to improve and increase personal productivity was such a powerful lure that people went out of their way to acquire PCs. They squeezed departmental budgets, bought them under the guise of typewriters, and even paid for them out of their own pockets.

Many companies that were slow to respond to this trend found that PC use was well established and flourishing among their competitors. In those companies, the Data Processing department was usually astounded to discover the extent of the PC invasion. The mainframe zealots were perhaps the most surprised to find out what was happening.

Seemingly overnight, the Data Processing department had lost control over a large percentage of the corporation's data. The territory they thought was theirs had been whittled away. What was perhaps most disturbing to them was that PC users were talking about information, not just raw data!

What users had discovered was that they could massage data and get what they wanted out of it. If they wanted a report, they could produce one that focused on their concerns. On the other hand, if they asked the DP group for a report, they would just get the standard reports that the mainframe generated. (It should also be noted that the standard report consumed a small forest in paper when all the user wanted was one page.)

A new trend developing was do-it-yourself computing. When users wanted to play what-if games with financial projections, they didn't have to come, hat in hand (metaphorically speaking), to the DP department. They could fire up their PCs and their spreadsheets and run through a dozen scenarios in the time it took DP to consider their requests.

There was also no way that DP could change the trend. The PC users were more productive. Corporations had every reason to support the trend and many reasons to be concerned with the anarchy that was building. As you'll see, the distribution of data throughout companies had many implications, and the greatest risk of all was loss of control.

More than any other factor, the PC revolution forced corporate data processing departments to rethink their role and their use of technology. They had no choice, really, so they bit the bullet and became management information services (MIS), information technology (IT), or some other name with the word "information" in it. They also had to embrace, or at least work with, the tidal wave of PC technology.

Getting Connected

In the days of CP/M, the cost of quality peripherals was exorbitant. A 14", 10MB hard disk drive that consumed 5 amps and sounded like a Lear jet taking off when it started was as expensive as the rest of the computer. A dot matrix printer that couldn't even begin to do near-letter-quality output was a precious resource. By the time the IBM PC was launched, prices had dropped but were still hefty. In short, PC resources were like gold: scarce and valuable.

It wasn't practical for each microcomputer to have hard disk storage and a printer, although without them a PC's productivity was limited. Another problem was that sharing data was also a pain. If you wanted to get a document that someone else had created, you had to take your floppy disk, put on your sneakers, and run over to the other microcomputer to get it. Hence the term for this kind of data sharing: *sneaker net.*

Sneaker Net

Sneaker net raised a lot of problems. How could you ensure that your documents were up-to-date if various copies, modified by any number of people, were all circulating on different disks? How could you stop documents from being stolen? What if the only up-to-date version was on a floppy disk and someone used the disk as a coffee coaster? What if… ?

There were a hundred problems with the sneaker net approach, and all of them pointed in the same direction: the need, the absolute necessity to pass the documents between computers electronically. Combine that need with the desirability of sharing expensive disk storage and printers, and you have a problem looking for a solution. It was this need to share data and peripherals that stimulated the creation of the first local area networks, but, as you shall see, the need to share data became the central issue.

Data Switches

One way for PCs to share peripherals was to use a data switch, a device that allowed one user at a time to use a device such as a printer. If another person was using the printer when you wanted to use it, you had to wait until they finished. A data switch could be compared to a line at the bank. Whichever person (data to be printed) gets to the line (the data switch) first gets to a teller (the printer) first. The others have to wait until the first is finished.

The data switch provided users with a serial or parallel port connection, and whoever sent data first got access to the printer. To relinquish control, a PC would have to send a specific character sequence to say, in effect, "I'm finished." (See Figure 1.5.)

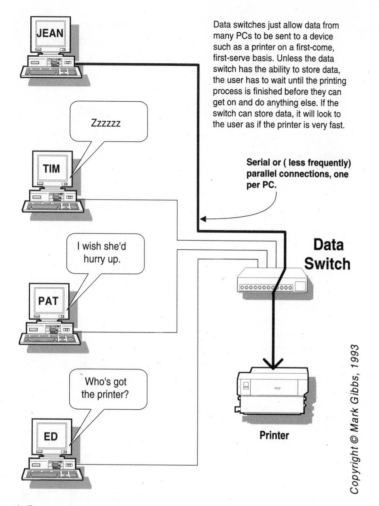

Figure 1.5.
PCs sharing a printer through a data switch.

Although these devices worked for printers and plotters (and still do—several companies still offer them) they didn't allow you to share hard disks. They also required a dedicated line to and from each PC to the switch. This could be clumsy if the PCs were far apart, and impossible if there were more than a few PCs involved.

Disks Served Here

The first attempt at what is now called local area networking (LAN) was a technology called disk servers, now pretty much obsolete. A disk server was a PC that, through some kind of communications technology, was linked to a group of *client* PCs. (See Figure 1.6.) It ran a special operating system that was designed to handle simultaneous file and printer access by multiple clients: a network operating system (NOS).

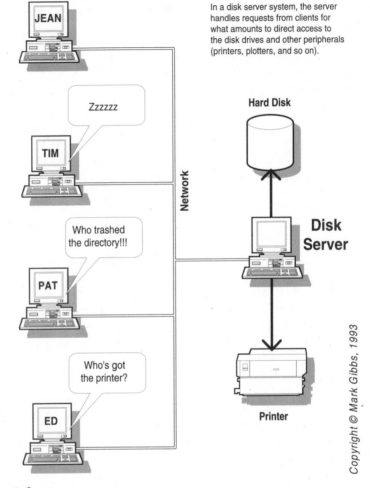

Figure 1.6.
A disk server system providing disk and printer resources to a group of PCs.

NOTE:

The computer business has always been a major generator of acronyms, but the communications division (to which networking belongs) is perhaps the greatest source of all. In fact, it has been suggested that the word "acronym" is itself an acronym for "All Computers Rely On Nearly crazY Messages."

The term *local area networks* originated as a description of size—they cover a small, local area, with a typical radius of no more than a mile or so. They also carry data at high speeds and are usually owned by a single organization. Metropolitan area networks (MANs) cover a city and operate at data rates similar to LANs.

The biggest networks of all, wide area networks (WANs), are worldwide services such as the CompuServe Information Services Network, and they typically operate at low speeds (although that is now changing).

Both MANs and WANs are usually owned by service companies that resell the data service to end-users. (This also applies to the Internet, which we'll discuss later.) However, the dividing lines between the various types are blurring as MAN and WAN services approach LAN speeds.

Defining Our Terms

Before I explain the way a disk server was used, I need to establish some terms, some of which are illustrated in Figure 1.7:

✖ *Reading* data is the operation that retrieves the text you entered on a word processor and saved in a document (a file), for example. The same term also applies to getting a record from a database or retrieving a drawing from a file. *Writing* is the process of putting data into files.

✖ A *sector* is a chunk of information on a hard or floppy disk. A sector can contain anything from 256 bytes of data on a floppy disk all the way up to 2,048 bytes or more on a hard disk used on a network.

✖ A *block* is a number of sectors on a hard or floppy disk.

✖ A *track* is a group of sectors on a hard disk or a floppy disk.

✖ A *head* is a component that reads and writes data on floppy disks or hard disks. An individual head is used for every disk surface, and a disk *platter* has two surfaces. A disk with eight heads has eight surfaces on four platters.

✖ A *physical drive* is, of course, a real, kickable hard disk or floppy disk drive. (Kicking a drive that is in working order is not to be advised—they're expensive and usually useful. If it breaks, and if you feel so inclined, go ahead and kick it. However, this is also not recommended because they're pretty heavy; punting a drive more than six inches is a feat suitable only for Arnold Schwarzenegger wearing Doc Martins.)

✖ A *logical drive* is simply a way of looking at a physical drive. If you have a large hard disk drive and it's divided into two parts (one part accessible as drive C:, one part as drive D:), you are seeing the physical drive from a logical viewpoint. C: and D: are called logical drives. A logical view makes it easier to organize a disk. In fact, it may be necessary to divide a very large disk into two or more parts because the operating system may be incapable of handling a single huge drive.

✖ A *file* is nothing more than a collection of sectors on a disk that has been set aside to store data.

✖ A *directory* is like a folder in a file cabinet (which can be thought of as equivalent to a logical drive). Files (like documents) contain data and are stored in directories (folders). Directories can also contain other directories, just as folders can contain both documents and other folders.

✖ On a network, *resources* that are on another computer but that you can use as if they were on your own are a logical view of physical things such as floppy disks, hard disks, and printers.

✖ A *device* refers to a logical or physical resource.

✖ A *local* device or resource is attached to your PC.

✖ A *remote* device or resource is on another computer that is accessed across a network or other communication system.

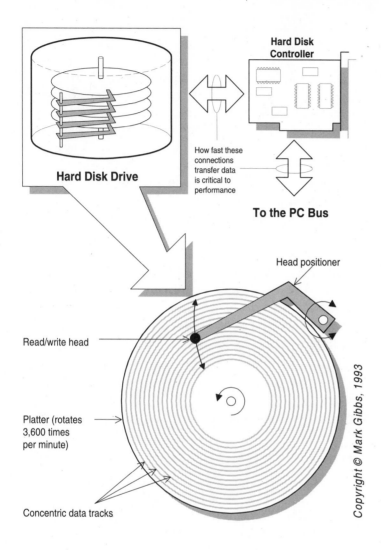

Figure 1.7.
The important information about disk drives.

Clue: *Physical* and *logical* are terms that often pop up in computer technology. For example, a librarian can look things up for you in a set of encyclopedias. To find the article on bungee jumping, you can ask the librarian to turn to Volume 2, page 40. This is a physical request because you're looking for data directly at its real, physical location. If you were to say, "Look up bungee jumping," however, you would be making a logical request. The librarian would need to translate your logical request into a physical location. This would obviously be easier for you because the librarian would do the work of translation for you—you wouldn't need a detailed knowledge of the encyclopedia's layout.

If you look at a computer as a library, the disk storage system (that is, hard or floppy disks) as an encyclopedia, the operating system as the librarian, and the program as yourself, you can see that life is much simpler for the program if logical requests are used. You (the program) can go to different libraries (computers) where different encyclopedias (storage systems) are used, and you (the program) can find the same information if the same type of librarian (operating system) is used.

A logical interpretation of a physical thing is a trick to make it easier to use. With hard and floppy disk drives, it's a lot easier to ask for block 276 (a logical request) than to ask for track 12, head 4, sectors 3, 4, and 5 (a physical request). In the latter case, you need to know exactly how the disk is laid out.

Exactly What Is a Disk Server?

With a disk server, programs running on a client PC can read and write to what the program sees as a local, logical disk resource. What is important in this situation is that the client does all of the housekeeping. For example, when a file is opened to be read, the client reads the directory information describing what files are where, interprets the information, finds where the file is, and reads data from the file. In a file server system, the requests ("Read the directory information" and "Read the file contents") are carried out by the server's operating system as requests to read sectors. The server has no idea what the sectors actually contain; it just does what it's told to do.

This is where problems set in. Disk servers can restrict user access to an entire data area, but can't control how a directory area or a file is used. This means that a user can be prevented from having any access at all, allowed to only read data, or not allowed to do anything. It is impossible, for example, to give clients the ability to read and write to files but prevent them from deleting files. If the client operating system of a disk server is able to do anything that could change a file or directory, it has to have total access. The operations that can cause changes are as follows:

✖ Adding data to a file
✖ Changing file data
✖ Creating a new file
✖ Deleting an existing file
✖ Renaming a file
✖ Creating a subdirectory
✖ Deleting a subdirectory
✖ Renaming a subdirectory

This means that a disk server client could trash (the hip term for corrupting) a file or even wipe the directory clean, and therefore delete all files and subdirectories.

Another problem is that sharing data on disk server systems is difficult. Unless programs running on different clients have a reliable way of coordinating their access to information in a file, one program can overwrite another program's changes without knowing it. For example, suppose that Mr. and Mrs. B are out shopping. Mr. B is at the Rolls Royce dealership and wants to buy a car, while Mrs. B is at the boat showroom to buy a yacht. Both salesmen want to check that the Bs have adequate credit available on their credit cards, and they both contact the credit card company at the same time. The first operator checks the Bs' account and finds they have $200,000 credit available, so Mr. B. can buy his $120,000 car. The second operator simultaneously does the same for Mrs. B's $140,000 yacht. The first operator now deducts the purchase from the available credit line and the Bs' account is updated to show an $80,000 credit line. The other operator does the same thing and overwrites the other operator's changes, leaving the account with $60,000 credit when, in fact, it is now overdrawn by $60,000!

The solution to this is to use some form of record or file locking. You need to be able to say, in effect, "I'm using the Bs' record" or "I'm using the credit accounts file." Because the disk server system doesn't know what data you're using, you must rely on some form of coordination that you have both agreed to beforehand. This means that if a program that isn't part of the locking scheme accesses the file, the information can be corrupted.

> **NOTE:**
> A *record* is a group of bytes (characters) in a file. Fixed-length records are those in which each record has the same number of characters. In variable-length records, each record can have a different number of characters. The records are separated by terminator characters, such as at the start of a new line. In a database with fixed-length records, each record has the same layout. If you want the 10th record and each record is 100 characters long, you start reading at the 1,001st byte. If the records are not of equal length, or you want to go directly to a record, you need an index file. The index file gives you the number of the first byte of the required record without requiring you to read through the file until you find what you want.

Yet another problem exists (just when you thought it couldn't get worse). If a client is updating information in a file or adding information to it (that is, making the file longer—also called extending) and, for some reason, stops working (because the PC is reset, or because of a software problem, failure of the network system, or power failure), the housekeeping data necessary to describe the file will be lost or scrambled. Because of the complexity of requiring all clients to manage the directory data, the problems of failure are, as they say, nontrivial. If the client locks a record and then fails, that record will probably be unavailable until some kind of special operator interaction is taken.

Disk server systems did a lot of business and established the market for today's vendors. But disk server technology was an interim step between simple device sharing systems and the file server technology that was to come. Today, 10-year-old disk server systems can still be found earning their keep in major companies, but their days are numbered.

The Next Step for Servers

There were two reasons that disk servers came first in the relentless march of networking technology: ease of implementation and hardware limitations. A disk server system is one of the easiest resource sharing systems to implement. All of the hard work of controlling the environment and coordinating multiple PCs that use the same data areas has to be done by applications if it is to be done at anything more than a primitive level.

```
● Mark Gibbs, 1992                                       Form: DIY-008
                          Network Configuration
                     Acme Secretarial Services, Inc.
```

Location	Type	Function	Machine name
Manager	C/S	Document database	LUCY
Sec. 1	C		JEAN
Sec. 2	C		PAT
Sec. 3	C		GLAEN
Recep. 1	C		ED
Recep. 2	C		BRENNEN
Print/archive	SO	Mail, mailing database print, and archives	GRYPHON

```
Prepared by:              Date:              Page:
            L.R. Smith              3/16/1992        1   of  1
```
```
     This form is taken from "Do-It-Yourself Networking With LANtastic"
                      Published by SAMS (1992)
```

Figure 13.12.
Acme's general network configuration.

Naming Machines on the Network

How you name the PCs on your network is pretty much up to you. You can choose names based on the name of the normal user of that PC (such as "mgibbs"), or you can give the machine its own name (such as "Server 3").

In general, you should name the machines as is appropriate for your organization's needs. If your company is very formal, it may be inappropriate to call a server "Snoopy" or "Bigboy." And unless you want to make casual network access difficult, names should also be reasonably easy to remember and should relate to their function. For example, a server called "T$R_PP" would not be easy to identify.

Workstation, Workstation/Server, or Server Only?

If you want to have the greatest degree of access to all network resources, you may decide to make every user's machine a workstation/server. Although this means access is always available, it increases the number of servers that need to be managed. By the time you have 10 or 20 servers running, you may regret such a decision.

> **NOTE:**
>
> On peer-to-peer networks, it's usually the case that if you configure PCs with users on them as workstations only, you will use less memory. This can be a crucial issue with many of today's applications, which just get fatter and fatter (that is, use more RAM) with each release. Why, when I was a boy we could get an entire word processor on 32 kilobytes and write whole books on a single floppy disk. Ah, those were the days... NOT!

To increase performance with LANtastic, you can make a PC a dedicated server by running the ALONE.EXE program. This is also a wise idea when there's any chance of a casual user interfering with or, even worse, disrupting the service supplied by the server. ALONE can be "locked" to prevent unauthorized access. (Of course, nothing beats locking servers away in a cupboard or storeroom to ensure that they're secure.)

> **NOTE:**
>
> If you do decide to lock your computers away so that they can't be interfered with, do ensure that the cupboard or room is well-ventilated, doesn't overheat in summer, doesn't overheat in the winter (when the heating is on), doesn't have water pipes running through it over the computers, has a smoke detector, is easily accessed in case of fire, and is "up to code." Don't let this list put you off. It's just that if you're making the investment of time and money to build a useful network, you want it to be reliable and safe.

What Functions Will Each Server Have?

Many people tend to load as many functions as possible onto a single server system. The usual result is a decrease in performance (which you can buy your way out of to a great extent, but that's not an option for everyone) and an increase in complexity, neither of which are probably what was intended.

In general, try to spread the work among all of the servers. Don't use one server for all of the databases, archiving, and printing if you have other servers that can sensibly share the load.

If a server is in fact a workstation/server and has a user on it, try to avoid making that system a focus for many users; otherwise, all users will see a drop in performance.

Configuring the Servers

Once you've established the general layout and configuration of the network, you need to do a detailed configuration for each server. This should cover:

✖ General setup

✖ Server's resources

✖ Server's users

Figures 13.13 and 13.14 show the configurations of Acme's two server systems: GRYPHON (the print, database, and archive server) and LUCY (the office manager's PC, which will hold the document templates).

General Setup

You'll notice that the mail system has been disabled on LUCY because Lucy wanted all users to access just one mail system on GRYPHON. Once the servers were planned in outline, Acme could start developing a user configuration plan for both servers. (See Figures 13.15 and 13.16.)

```
 © Mark Gibbs, 1992                                          Form: DIY-009
                      Network Server Configuration #1
                        Acme Secretarial Services, Inc.

Server name       GRYPHON              Location         Main office
Control dir.      C:\LANTASTI.NET      Install dir.     C:\LANTASTI
Mail system       Enabled              Server user      None (dedicated)
Startup file      C:\LANTASTI\STARTNET.BAT merged into AUTOEXEC.BAT
Directory structure:

     C:\
            LANTASTI
            LANTASTI.NET      - etc.
            DOS
            APPS
            BACKUP
                   JEAN
                   PAT
                   GLAEN
                   ED
                   BRENNEN
                   LUCY
            ARCHIVES
                   QUOTES
                   REPORTS
            ACCOUNTS




Prepared by:              Date:                   Page:
            L.R. Smith                3/16/1992        1   of  1

     This form is taken from "Do-It-Yourself Networking With LANtastic"
                         Published by SAMS (1992)
```

Figure 13.13.
The planned configuration for Acme's server GRYPHON.

```
● Mark Gibbs, 1992                                          Form: DIY-009

                    Network Server Configuration #1

                     Acme Secretarial Services, Inc.
```

Server name	LUCY	Location	Main office
Control dir.	c:\LANTASTI.NET	Install dir.	C:\LANTASTI
Mail system	~~Enabled~~	Server user	None (dedicated)
Startup file	C:\LANTASTI\STARTNET.BAT merged into AUTOEXEC.BAT		

```
Directory structure:


      C:\
              LANTASTI
              LANTASTI.NET        - etc.
              DOS
              APPS
              ARCHIVES
                      QUOTES
                      REPORTS
              ACCOUNTS
              WORK
              WP
              DOCUMENT        - shared templates and files
```

Prepared by:	Date:	Page:
L.R. Smith	3/16/1992	1 of 1

```
         This form is taken from "Do-It-Yourself Networking With LANtastic"
                         Published by SAMS (1992)
```

Figure 13.14.

The planned configuration for Acme's server LUCY.

```
  ● Mark Gibbs, 1992                                          Form: DIY-010
                    Network Server Configuration #2: Users

                       Acme Secretarial Services, Inc.


                  ┌─────────────────┬───────────────────────┐
                  │ Server name     │ GRYPHON               │
                  └─────────────────┴───────────────────────┘
```

Real name		User name	* ("everyone")
Status	Group	Privileges	(none)
Acc. expiration	Never	Login days	M T W T F
Renew password	0 days	Login times	08:00 to 18:00
Real name	Lucy Smith	User name	LRSMITH
Status	System manger	Privileges	Q M U S
Acc. expiration	Never	Login days	S M T W T F S
Renew password	7 days	Login times	00:00 to 24:00
Real name	Jean Gibbs	User name	AJGIBBS
Status		Privileges	U
Acc. expiration	Never	Login days	M T W T F
Renew password	30 days	Login times	08:00 to 18:00
Real name	Pat Lay	User name	PLAY
Status		Privileges	U
Acc. expiration	Never	Login days	M T W T F
Renew password	30 days	Login times	08:00 to 18:00
Real name	Glaen Redeker	User name	GREDEKER
Status		Privileges	U
Acc. expiration	Never	Login days	M T W T F
Renew password	30 days	Login times	08:00 to 18:00
Real name	Ed Lay	User name	ELAY
Status	System manager	Privileges	Q M U S
Acc. expiration	Never	Login days	S M T W T F S
Renew password	7 days	Login times	00:00 to 24:00
Real name	Brennen Redeker	User name	BREDEKER
Status		Privileges	U
Acc. expiration	Never	Login days	M T W T F
Renew password	30 days	Login times	08:00 to 18:00

Prepared by:	Date:	Page:
L.R. Smith	3/16/1992	1 of 1

```
          This form is taken from "Do-It-Yourself Networking With LANtastic"
                            Published by SAMS (1992)
```

Figure 13.15.
The planned users and their configuration for Acme's server GRYPHON.

© Mark Gibbs, 1992

Form: DIY-010

Network Server Configuration #2: Users

Acme Secretarial Services, Inc.

Server name	LUCY

Real name		User name	* ("everyone")
Status	Group	Privileges	(none)
Acc. expiration	Never	Login days	M T W T F
Renew password	0 days	Login times	08:00 to 18:00
Real name	Lucy Smith	User name	LRSMITH
Status	System manger	Privileges	Q M U S
Acc. expiration	Never	Login days	S M T W T F S
Renew password	7 days	Login times	00:00 to 24:00
Real name	Jean Gibbs	User name	AJGIBBS
Status		Privileges	U
Acc. expiration	Never	Login days	M T W T F
Renew password	30 days	Login times	08:00 to 18:00
Real name	Pat Lay	User name	PLAY
Status		Privileges	U
Acc. expiration	Never	Login days	M T W T F
Renew password	30 days	Login times	08:00 to 18:00
Real name	Glaen Redeker	User name	GREDEKER
Status		Privileges	U
Acc. expiration	Never	Login days	M T W T F
Renew password	30 days	Login times	08:00 to 18:00
Real name	Ed Lay	User name	ELAY
Status	System manager	Privileges	Q M U S
Acc. expiration	Never	Login days	S M T W T F S
Renew password	7 days	Login times	00:00 to 24:00
Real name	Brennen Redeker	User name	BREDEKER
Status		Privileges	U
Acc. expiration	Never	Login days	M T W T F
Renew password	30 days	Login times	08:00 to 18:00

Prepared by:	Date:		Page:	
L.R. Smith		3/16/1992	1	of 1

This form is taken from "Do-It-Yourself Networking With LANtastic"
Published by SAMS (1992)

Figure 13.16.

The planned users and their configuration for Acme's server LUCY.

Server Resources

Next, each server's shared resources had to be planned. For GRYPHON, Acme's plan for shared disk resources is shown in Figure 13.17, and their plan for shared printers is shown in Figures 13.18, 13.19, and 13.20. The shared disk resources for LUCY are shown in Figure 13.21. (LUCY wasn't intended to have any printers attached, so there's no shared printer resource plan.)

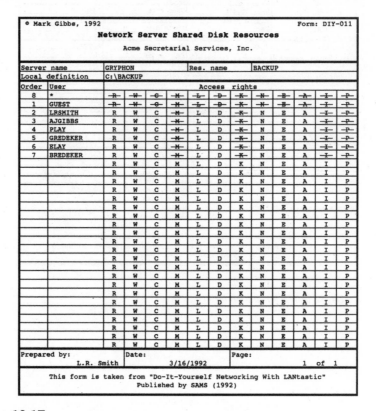

Figure 13.17.
The configuration of shared disk resources on Acme's server GRYPHON.

```
© Mark Gibbs, 1992                                    Form: DIY-012
              Network Server Shared Printer Resources
                   Acme Secretarial Services, Inc.
```

Server name	GRYPHON					Resource name		@LASER1			
Printer	Apple LaserWriter II NT										
Port	COM1:	~~COM2:~~		~~LPT1:~~		~~LPT2:~~		~~LPT3:~~			
Baud rate	9600					Banner		ENABLED			
Form feeds	DISABLED					Lines/page		DISABLED			
Immed. despool	ENABLED					Despool timeout		60		seconds	
Tab width	0					Paper width		80			
Chars/second	0					Handshake		H/W	S/W	None	
Setup delay	0					Cleanup delay		0			

Order	User	Access rights (R WCL are standard)										
8	*	R	W	C	~~M~~	L	~~D~~	~~K~~	~~N~~	~~E~~	~~A~~	~~I~~	~~P~~
1	GUEST	R	W	C	~~M~~	L	~~D~~	~~K~~	~~N~~	~~E~~	~~A~~	~~I~~	~~P~~
2	LRSMITH	R	W	C	~~M~~	L	~~D~~	~~K~~	~~N~~	~~E~~	~~A~~	~~I~~	~~P~~
3	AJGIBBS	R	W	C	~~M~~	L	~~D~~	~~K~~	~~N~~	~~E~~	~~A~~	~~I~~	~~P~~
4	PLAY	R	W	C	~~M~~	L	~~D~~	~~K~~	~~N~~	~~E~~	~~A~~	~~I~~	~~P~~
5	GREDEKER	R	W	C	~~M~~	L	~~D~~	~~K~~	~~N~~	~~E~~	~~A~~	~~I~~	~~P~~
6	ELAY	R	W	C	~~M~~	L	~~D~~	~~K~~	~~N~~	~~E~~	~~A~~	~~I~~	~~P~~
7	BREDEKER	R	W	C	~~M~~	L	~~D~~	~~K~~	~~N~~	~~E~~	~~A~~	~~I~~	~~P~~
		R	W	C	M	L	D	K	N	E	A	I	P
		R	W	C	M	L	D	K	N	E	A	I	P
		R	W	C	M	L	D	K	N	E	A	I	P
		R	W	C	M	L	D	K	N	E	A	I	P
		R	W	C	M	L	D	K	N	E	A	I	P
		R	W	C	M	L	D	K	N	E	A	I	P
		R	W	C	M	L	D	K	N	E	A	I	P
		R	W	C	M	L	D	K	N	E	A	I	P
		R	W	C	M	L	D	K	N	E	A	I	P
		R	W	C	M	L	D	K	N	E	A	I	P
		R	W	C	M	L	D	K	N	E	A	I	P
		R	W	C	M	L	D	K	N	E	A	I	P
		R	W	C	M	L	D	K	N	E	A	I	P
		R	W	C	M	L	D	K	N	E	A	I	P

Prepared by: L.R. Smith	Date: 3/16/1992	Page: 1 of 1

```
This form is taken from "Do-It-Yourself Networking With LANtastic"
                  Published by SAMS (1992)
```

Figure 13.18.

The configuration of shared printer resource @LASER1 on Acme's server GRYPHON.

© Mark Gibbs, 1992										Form: DIY-012

Network Server Shared Printer Resources

Acme Secretarial Services, Inc.

Server name	GRYPHON					Resource name		@LASER2		
Printer	HP Laserjet II									
Port		COM1:	COM2:		LPT1:		LPT2:		LPT3:	
Baud rate				Banner			ENABLED			
Form feeds	ENABLED			Lines/page			DISABLED			
Immed. despool	ENABLED			Despool timeout			60		seconds	
Tab width	0			Paper width			80			
Chars/second	0			Handshake			H/W S/W None			
Setup delay	0			Cleanup delay			0			

Order	User	Access rights (R WCL are standard)									
8	*	R	W	C	M	L	D	K	N	E	A	I	P
1	GUEST	R	W	C	M	L	D	K	N	E	A	I	P
2	LRSMITH	R	W	C	M	L	D	K	N	E	A	I	P
3	AJGIBBS	R	W	C	M	L	D	K	N	E	A	I	P
4	PLAY	R	W	C	M	L	D	K	N	E	A	I	P
5	GREDEKER	R	W	C	M	L	D	K	N	E	A	I	P
6	ELAY	R	W	C	M	L	D	K	N	E	A	I	P
7	BREDEKER	R	W	C	M	L	D	K	N	E	A	I	P
		R	W	C	M	L	D	K	N	E	A	I	P
		R	W	C	M	L	D	K	N	E	A	I	P
		R	W	C	M	L	D	K	N	E	A	I	P
		R	W	C	M	L	D	K	N	E	A	I	P
		R	W	C	M	L	D	K	N	E	A	I	P
		R	W	C	M	L	D	K	N	E	A	I	P
		R	W	C	M	L	D	K	N	E	A	I	P
		R	W	C	M	L	D	K	N	E	A	I	P
		R	W	C	M	L	D	K	N	E	A	I	P
		R	W	C	M	L	D	K	N	E	A	I	P
		R	W	C	M	L	D	K	N	E	A	I	P
		R	W	C	M	L	D	K	N	E	A	I	P
		R	W	C	M	L	D	K	N	E	A	I	P

Prepared by:	Date:	Page:
L.R. Smith	3/16/1992	1 of 1

This form is taken from "Do-It-Yourself Networking With LANtastic"
Published by SAMS (1992)

Figure 13.19.

The configuration of shared printer resource @LASER2 on Acme's server GRYPHON.

⊕ Mark Gibbs, 1992								Form: DIY-012			
Network Server Shared Printer Resources											
Acme Secretarial Services, Inc.											
Server name	GRYPHON				Resource name			@DOTMATRIX			
Printer	EPSON FX-100										
Port		~~COM1:~~	~~COM2:~~		~~LPT1:~~		LPT2:		~~LPT3:~~		
Baud rate					Banner			ENABLED			
Form feeds	ENABLED				Lines/page			60			
Immed. despool	ENABLED				Despool timeout			60		seconds	
Tab width	0				Paper width			80			
Chars/second	0				Handshake			H/W	S/W	None	
Setup delay	0				Cleanup delay			0			
Order	User	Access rights (R WCL are standard)									
8	*	R	W	C	~~M~~	L	~~D~~	~~K~~	~~N~~	~~E~~	~~A~~	~~I~~	~~P~~
1	GUEST	R	W	C	~~M~~	L	~~D~~	~~K~~	~~N~~	~~E~~	~~A~~	~~I~~	~~P~~
2	LRSMITH	R	W	C	~~M~~	L	~~D~~	~~K~~	~~N~~	~~E~~	~~A~~	~~I~~	~~P~~
3	AJGIBBS	R	W	C	~~M~~	L	~~D~~	~~K~~	~~N~~	~~E~~	~~A~~	~~I~~	~~P~~
4	PLAY	R	W	C	~~M~~	L	~~D~~	~~K~~	~~N~~	~~E~~	~~A~~	~~I~~	~~P~~
5	GREDEKER	R	W	C	~~M~~	L	~~D~~	~~K~~	~~N~~	~~E~~	~~A~~	~~I~~	~~P~~
6	ELAY	R	W	C	~~M~~	L	~~D~~	~~K~~	~~N~~	~~E~~	~~A~~	~~I~~	~~P~~
7	BREDEKER	R	W	C	~~M~~	L	~~D~~	~~K~~	~~N~~	~~E~~	~~A~~	~~I~~	~~P~~
		R	W	C	M	L	D	K	N	E	A	I	P
		R	W	C	M	L	D	K	N	E	A	I	P
		R	W	C	M	L	D	K	N	E	A	I	P
		R	W	C	M	L	D	K	N	E	A	I	P
		R	W	C	M	L	D	K	N	E	A	I	P
		R	W	C	M	L	D	K	N	E	A	I	P
		R	W	C	M	L	D	K	N	E	A	I	P
		R	W	C	M	L	D	K	N	E	A	I	P
		R	W	C	M	L	D	K	N	E	A	I	P
		R	W	C	M	L	D	K	N	E	A	I	P
		R	W	C	M	L	D	K	N	E	A	I	P
		R	W	C	M	L	D	K	N	E	A	I	P
		R	W	C	M	L	D	K	N	E	A	I	P
Prepared by: L.R. Smith		Date: 3/16/1992					Page:		1 of 1		
This form is taken from "Do-It-Yourself Networking With LANtastic" Published by SAMS (1992)											

Figure 13.20.

The configuration of shared printer resource @DOTMATRIX on Acme's server GRYPHON.

Mark Gibbs, 1992											Form: DIY-011

Network Server Shared Disk Resources

Acme Secretarial Services, Inc.

Server name	LUCY					Res. name		DOCUMENT			
Local definition	C:\WP\DOCUMENT										
Order	User					Access rights					
8	*	~~R~~	~~W~~	~~C~~	~~M~~	~~L~~	~~D~~	~~K~~	~~N~~	~~E~~	~~A~~	~~I~~	~~P~~
1	GUEST	~~R~~	~~W~~	~~C~~	~~M~~	~~L~~	~~D~~	~~K~~	~~N~~	~~E~~	~~A~~	~~I~~	~~P~~
2	LRSMITH	R	~~W~~	~~C~~	~~M~~	L	~~D~~	~~K~~	~~N~~	~~E~~	~~A~~	~~I~~	~~P~~
3	AJGIBBS	R	~~W~~	~~C~~	~~M~~	L	~~D~~	~~K~~	~~N~~	~~E~~	~~A~~	~~I~~	~~P~~
4	PLAY	R	~~W~~	~~C~~	~~M~~	L	~~D~~	~~K~~	~~N~~	~~E~~	~~A~~	~~I~~	~~P~~
5	GREDEKER	R	~~W~~	~~C~~	~~M~~	L	~~D~~	~~K~~	~~N~~	~~E~~	~~A~~	~~I~~	~~P~~
6	ELAY	R	~~W~~	~~C~~	~~M~~	L	~~D~~	~~K~~	~~N~~	~~E~~	~~A~~	~~I~~	~~P~~
7	BREDEKER	R	~~W~~	~~C~~	~~M~~	L	~~D~~	~~K~~	~~N~~	~~E~~	~~A~~	~~I~~	~~P~~
		R	W	C	M	L	D	K	N	E	A	I	P
		R	W	C	M	L	D	K	N	E	A	I	P
		R	W	C	M	L	D	K	N	E	A	I	P
		R	W	C	M	L	D	K	N	E	A	I	P
		R	W	C	M	L	D	K	N	E	A	I	P
		R	W	C	M	L	D	K	N	E	A	I	P
		R	W	C	M	L	D	K	N	E	A	I	P
		R	W	C	M	L	D	K	N	E	A	I	P
		R	W	C	M	L	D	K	N	E	A	I	P
		R	W	C	M	L	D	K	N	E	A	I	P
		R	W	C	M	L	D	K	N	E	A	I	P
		R	W	C	M	L	D	K	N	E	A	I	P
		R	W	C	M	L	D	K	N	E	A	I	P
		R	W	C	M	L	D	K	N	E	A	I	P
		R	W	C	M	L	D	K	N	E	A	I	P
		R	W	C	M	L	D	K	N	E	A	I	P
		R	W	C	M	L	D	K	N	E	A	I	P
		R	W	C	M	L	D	K	N	E	A	I	P
		R	W	C	M	L	D	K	N	E	A	I	P

Prepared by:	Date:	Page:
L.R. Smith	3/16/1992	1 of 1

This form is taken from "Do-It-Yourself Networking With LANtastic" Published by SAMS (1992)

Figure 13.21.
The configuration of shared disk resources on Acme's server LUCY.

The Timetable

Now that you've planned your network, what you'll need to purchase, and how it will be organized, you can start to build a *timetable*. This is simply a schedule of what will be done, when it will be done, and who'll do it.

It's vitally important that you don't rush any stage of the installation process. Haste does indeed make waste, as well as mistakes. For example, when you don't allow adequate time for installing the network adapters, a small problem such as having trouble fitting a card into a slot or trying to retrieve a screw that has fallen into the PC can delay you so that you're still rushing around like a lunatic at midnight.

A strategy that can pay off if you're not in a tearing hurry to get the network running (which, according to Murphy, will not work properly under that constraint) is to break the installation process into several small steps and upgrade one PC each session. It's important to ensure that when the network goes into active service, it works properly. If it doesn't, the users may not take the network seriously or may avoid using it because of the potential consequences of its failures. This lack of user confidence will not help integrate the network into the organization, and will certainly delay the benefits of the system.

NOTE:

Murphy's law of time states, "The time required to complete a task is at least twice the time allocated, if you're in a hurry."

Gibbs' Addendum states, "If the task is *urgent*, it will take twice as long as it would have if you'd only been in a hurry."

A timetable should cover the following events:

- ✖ **Ordering equipment.** This includes getting quotes and placing the order.
- ✖ **Receiving and checking equipment.** When the equipment arrives, you need to make sure that the packages aren't damaged and that what the supplier marks as being sent on the packing note is actually there. The larger the network is, the more important checking equipment becomes.
- ✖ **Reading manuals and checking plans.** Although you may have made detailed plans, when you read the manuals that come with the products you may find that there are changes to software configuration or hardware settings. Allowing time to validate your plans can save a lot of time in the actual installation.
- ✖ **Site preparation.** In addition to installing cable, it's likely that you'll have to move furniture, check or upgrade power supplies, and so on.
- ✖ **Hardware installation.** As has already been said, there are two ways to schedule installing hardware: all at once or spread over a few days or weeks. For larger networks, installation over a period of time is often the only choice. If you have a smaller network, or if you're new to working on PC hardware, make sure that you take your time.
- ✖ **Software installation.** As with the other phases, give yourself adequate time. If you're going to make major changes, such as moving data from one PC to another, make backups first in case you have a problem or make a mistake.

✖ **Configuring and testing.** Configuring and testing can be a long process. This process will be shorter if you do the kind of planning discussed here, but again, you must not rush it. Testing, in particular, must be thorough. Correcting problems that occur when users are trying to do their jobs is always frustrating and stressful for all concerned.

✖ **Going "live."** A target date should be set for the network to become operational. By this date, all planned facilities should be tested and working correctly. For larger networks, you might phase in the introduction of services over a period of time. This allows users to become familiar with facilities one at a time, and reduces the time that the system is out of commission while it's being configured.

✖ **Training.** Although the network should be *transparent* (that is, it should not interfere with or be obvious to users), users will need instruction in the services that they can control. At the very minimum, users should be aware of the network and what it does for the company. This is good for building confidence in the system, and makes it more likely that any problems will be reported.

NOTE:

A great way to train users is to do it during a company-supplied pizza lunch—that'll usually get 'em to attend. Champagne and caviar also work pretty good, too.

The timetable that Lucy Smith drew up for Acme is shown in Figure 13.22.

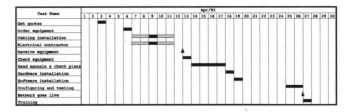

Figure 13.22.
Acme's network installation timetable.

Getting Sign-Off

You've reached the point at which you should have a case either for or against the proposed network. The viability of the plan will almost certainly be based on your financial argument—does the plan make financial sense for the company?

The proposal that Lucy Smith took to the owners was based on an analysis of the problems, their monetary consequences, and the projected savings that would result from solving those problems.

Although the approach you take to building a cost-justification argument for a network may vary from the Acme example, there is a common set of rules to follow. Remember the following six rules when you're seeking approval for introducing networking into your organization:

✖ **Avoid issues that have unquantifiable benefits.** Just saying that a network will make business more efficient doesn't provide a basis for a yes-or-no decision. The alternative is to say that, for example, turnaround on jobs will be 50% faster and job profitability will increase by 25%. This kind of argument will be very easy to agree to, provided your figures are verifiable.

✖ **Avoid technical discussions.** Very few people are interested in, or can understand, the technical issues of networking. Keep your proposal grounded in business issues.

✖ **Make sure that time frames are realistic—preferably pessimistic.** Don't tie yourself to an implementation schedule that will be difficult to achieve. Err on the side of caution. (And remember Murphy's Law of Contingent Failure—"If something can go wrong, it will.")

✖ **Keep it relevant.** Adding features or facilities that aren't relevant to business not only is of no interest to those who can sign off on the proposal, but it may detract from the perceived value of the system.

> **NOTE:**
>
> To get your hot little hands on features or facilities that aren't relevant to business but are things that you'd like to include, just slip 'em in under some other budgeted item. (But I didn't tell you that—I have a reputation to protect...)

✖ **Address reliability and security.** Most decision-makers will look for problems that are implicit in a proposal. The possibility and consequences of network failure or unauthorized access need to be considered and covered adequately. For smaller, less critical networks, this probably won't be a big issue, but it's still worth addressing in order to ensure that you have a plan for dealing with problems.

✖ **Assess risks.** Again, decision-makers are usually not keen on taking risks if they'll ultimately have to take responsibility. As you develop your plans, you'll see areas of risk. For example, if you hit a major obstacle during installation, what will the consequences be? How would you recover from problems? These issues are easily handled if you plan for them and address them in your proposal.

Management

The final part of your planning is defining the management activities that you'll be doing. An invaluable tool for developing a management strategy is establishing and maintaining a *system log*. This is simply a folder, box, or filing cabinet (it will depend on the size of the network) that contains as much information as possible about the network, how it was built, where the equipment and software was purchased, who installed it, and so on. You'll find that a well-organized and exhaustive system log is incredibly valuable when you get into hassles over warranties, software licenses, and responsibility for doing work.

Where and how you keep the system log information is up to you, but if you keep it on a computer, make sure that you have at least one easily accessible backup copy. An additional paper copy is also a good idea in case you can't access a computer-based copy.

WARNING:

In the spring of 1994, I gave a series of lectures on networking in eleven cities around the U.S. At each of the 23 lectures, I asked the network managers (totalling about 350) whether they had a system log. Altogether, only about 10 did—that's under 3 percent! Yet all of them had problems in managing their networks.

The fact is, the only way to keep a system log accurate is to start when the network is small. By the time it gets big, you'll be spending so much time adding new computers and sorting out problems that you won't have time to even start a log.

You have been warned.

The table of contents for the system log might look like this:

✖ **Section 1: Plans.** All of the plans, notes, and design work should be kept here for future reference.

✖ **Section 2: Equipment.** It's important to keep track of the equipment that makes up your network. You should log the details of the PCs (make, purchase information, configuration), network adapter cards (supplier, serial number, configuration, PC it's installed in), printers (supplier, serial number, configuration, PC it's attached to), and so on.

✖ **Section 3: Current configuration.** This section should contain all of your notes and any forms dealing with the current configuration of the network.

✖ **Section 4: Activities.** Because of the importance of your networked resources, maintaining them is vital to ensuring continued service. This section should contain your backup plan (what gets backed up, when, and to what device), restore plan (how backed-up data will be restored), how names will be generated, how passwords will be generated, and where they'll be kept in case they're lost (preferably under lock and key and in someone's charge). Do not keep the passwords in the system log!

✖ **Section 5: Logs.** If you do have a backup plan, you should keep track of when backups are done, who does them, and what storage system those backups are on. Similarly, restores should be recorded.

Summing Up How to Build Your Network

Although this whole formal planning and execution process may seem to be over-kill, particularly for small networks, it's likely that your network will grow either in size (connecting more PCs) or in importance to the organization (becoming critical to efficient business operation).

You'll find that the forms you use will make the task of planning and documenting your network much easier. And by creating and maintaining a system log, you'll be able to deal with any eventuality—from handling problems and failures to coping with expansion.

Doing a lot of planning before you get into the nuts and bolts of building a network will save you time and make your system much more cost-effective.

What Have You Learned?

1. The basic steps of a strategic network plan:

    Analyzing your needs.

    Doing a site analysis.

    Coming up with a basic design.

    Selecting the equipment.

    Creating a detailed configuration plan.

    Creating a timetable.

    Getting sign-offs (if required).

    Planning the management tasks.

2. The need for a network is usually created by one or more organizational or operational issues that can't be solved easily without using some method of intercommunication between PCs.

3. Five key problem areas that networking can address:

    Sharing the cost of expensive peripherals.

    Centralizing facilities to improve their manageability.

    Simplifying tasks by automation.

    Improving reliability by automation.

    Making better use of existing facilities.

4. The most effective business argument for a network is one based on filthy lucre (in other words, money). Remember, Gibbs' Golden Rule of Information Technology states "If it don't make money and it don't save money, it ain't *it*."

5. The relationship between cost and performance is that the more you pay, the faster you go. That's until you reach the technical performance "ceiling," after which you can pay as much as you like and you won't go

any faster. As Scotty said to ol' James T. Kirk on *Star Trek*, "You canna break th' laws o' physics, Captain."

6. The service load should be spread over as many servers as possible so that each can deliver the greatest performance possible.

7. A system log is simply a folder, box, or filing cabinet (it depends on the size of the network) that contains as much information as possible about the network, how it was built, where the equipment and software were purchased, who installed it, and so on. The system log helps you sort out problems such as when a warranty ran out, whether you're licensed for 200 copies of Word for Windows, or who did that cable installation that just failed.

Security and Disaster Recovery 14

1. What ramifications can usernames have on security?

2. What are some of the different combinations that can be implemented with passwords?

3. Once you've established a user base, how do you control the things they can get into?

4. What piece of your hardware system is the most likely to fail, and what can you do about it?

5. Are there any other options for drive fault tolerance besides mirroring and duplexing?

6. Why do you need to back up your server to removable media if you're already mirroring your hard drive?

7. Do you need to do a full backup every time?

8. What do you do if the power goes out? Does it matter beyond that brief moment?

9. Memory errors cause your workstation to completely lock up. Is there a type of memory that can save your server from experiencing this same problem?

The subject of security and disaster recovery has been brought up time and time again in this book, but it hasn't really been discussed at length. What if something goes wrong? What if some dastardly culprit decides it's your turn to be the victim of his/her latest exploration? What if your hardware decides that today is as good as any to breach the great divide and leap to its death? Well, you need to consider these possibilities no matter how much you'd prefer to avoid them.

Security

Security has already been discussed in great detail throughout this book, but there are some less technical concepts that you may not have considered.

Server-Based Systems

Larger networks require you to know who has access to each peripheral and who has control over that access. All of the major server vendors' operating systems give you a strong suite of security tools, and there are some basic rules that apply to all of them. Since the specific security capabilities of these packages have already been discussed, the following section will focus on suggestions and warnings that will help you build a strong but easy-to-understand system.

The first level of security in server-based networking systems is user authentication. It's easy to lose yourself in the number of controls offered to you. On the most simplistic level is the username. When you're creating usernames, pick a format and try to be as consistent as possible. Examples: GSMITH or SMITHG for the user Greg Smith. Don't be tempted to use nicknames. They're fun, but if you're working with large number of users it may be tough to remember who "Toad" is. Keep usernames short. Remember that you may need to type these names over and over again. If you try to use full names or Social Security numbers, it could make for a long afternoon later on down the line.

Passwords

You must control passwords strictly, but this can come back to bite you. Passwords in Novell NetWare can be controlled to the point of harassment. You can force the user to have a password. You can impose a minimum length for it (the shorter the password, the easier it is for someone else to pick it up by watching the user type it in). You can force the user to change it after a certain number of days (the more often someone types the same password, the more likely someone else is to catch it). You can force the user to change it to something he's never used before (it defeats the purpose of changing the password if he only ever uses two words). If you require passwords to be changed, you can give the user a specific number of logins before he's locked out.

If you put all of these constraints on passwords, be prepared to babysit. Users will constantly come to you because they've waited too long to change their passwords and have been locked out, or they don't think it's fair that they can't use their dog's name as a password for the eighteenth time.

Controlled Environment

Users that log in can be given specific abilities that are tied to that username. They can be placed into a specific controlled environment (to protect the innocent). You can limit the times of the day that specific accounts can log in; this prevents users from sitting in the office and searching for things to break into during non-business hours. You can set an expiration date for a specific account; this enables you to establish temporary accounts for people involved in short-term projects without having to worry about removing the accounts later. You can force a user to log into a specific machine; this enables you to control the usage of your more powerful workstations and to possibly stop untrustworthy users from gaining access to a peripheral and copying your data to disk. Lastly, you can limit users to a certain number of concurrent connections; this is the "social butterfly" stopper. By doing this, you stop people from logging into several machines and walking away from them. This particular activity seems harmless, but it can be one of the biggest threats to your security. Anyone can walk up to one of the machines that has been left alone and gain access to your network.

File and Directory Security

Once the users have logged into the file server, the next level is file and directory security. This is handled in two ways. The most basic form of post-login security consists of attributes. The attributes of a file indicate whether it's read-only, hidden, or system, and these attributes become part of the presentation of that file to any user (even the supervisor). This form of security is available (in a simple fashion) even in DOS, but in a file server a more robust set of attributes exists, and not all users can make changes to those attributes.

The second form of post-login security consists of file and directory rights. Rights are placed in the user or group assignments so that users can do only those things you want them to do to a specific file or directory. The assignment of rights is controlled by the system configuration utility. The difference between rights and attributes can be explained by looking at the rights and attributes of people. If a man has green hair, it doesn't matter who looks at him, he still has green hair. In this case, green hair is an attribute (as well as a cry for help). Now, if a woman walks into the White House off the street and wants to speak to the President of the United States, she most likely will not be able to do so because she doesn't have the proper clearance (or *rights*, in network terms). But if that woman was the First Lady, she would have the necessary clearance to speak to the President.

Different combinations of rights and attributes can make your job easier or harder. Keep in mind that the simplest form of security is preventing the user from even seeing the file or directory in the first place. (If he doesn't know the Twinkie exists, he probably won't try to take it.) You can hide a file or directory by changing the attributes or rights. If you give a file the Hidden attribute no one can see it, but people can still use it, even if they don't know it. This may become difficult to manage because not even the supervisor can see it.

One approach to using rights involves not giving a specific user or group of users the FILE SCAN right to the file. This enables the proper users to see the file, but it won't even be presented in a directory to the unwanted users.

If you make your file and directory security plan too intricate, you can overcomplicate the issue. The idea here is to keep it as simple as possible without creating a security risk. You can lock the doors tightly, but if you keep having to open them to let people in, it defeats your purpose and creates a security risk. Just keep in mind that if you set too many rules, you may create more work for yourself. With that said, don't kid yourself; being too loose with your security may leave your system vulnerable to disgruntled employees or those that just want to cause mischief. Cover yourself.

Peer-to-Peer Systems

Peer-to-peer systems aren't a good choice for large networks, mainly because of the difficulty in managing security. Each machine has independent control over security; the more machines you add as servers, the more machines you have to track. When these networks exceed 5 to 10 units, the job becomes almost unmanageable.

Peer-to-peer networks have minimal security schemes because they aren't meant to be the keepers of the keys to the kingdom. Most often these systems are meant to help people cooperate with one another, and security is minimized to make this as simple as possible. Also, the users of these machines aren't expected to be the Einsteins of the industry, so if the peer-to-peer manufacturers made the issues involved in managing these systems too complicated, they would alienate their target audience.

The most basic level of control a user has is the ability to completely turn off the sharing of peripherals. With Apple Computer's System 7, the user can select the icon of the shared drive and choose Sharing from the File menu. A checkbox is displayed; if it's checked, that means to share this item and its contents. It just needs to be unchecked to turn it off. Both Personal NetWare and Workgroups for Windows (WFW) have similar features, but they aren't quite as up front.

If a user chooses to share an item, he has other choices to make. The first is deciding which specific users can access the device. In the WFW and Apple implementations, the users are all given login names and passwords to each specific machine. In the Personal NetWare implementation, the users are logged into the network as a whole, and then each user chooses who gets rights to his peripherals.

Users have fewer rights in peer-to-peer systems than in client/server systems. They can usually get the right to read a file, write to a file, or copy a file. You might suggest to your users that they each create a directory to store sharable items in, rather than sharing the entire hard drive. You may want to name the directories SHARED1, SHARED2, etc. That way, if John wants to get something from Jane's shared directory, he knows her directory is called SHARED2. They can even name it SHARED. This can prevent them from having to constantly monitor what they're keeping on their drives and who has access.

Printer sharing is different in peer-to-peer systems. With Apple System 7, the user has no control over whether she'll share a printer located at her station. This is because Apple printers control their own network access. With DOS/Windows-based systems, the user has just two choices in this category: share it or don't.

Security for these systems requires that you be at the workstation in question in order to make the change you want to make. The more systems you have, the more work it takes to manage the total system. It's hard enough to find a needle in *a* haystack, let alone *fifteen* haystacks.

Hopefully this hasn't soured you on the idea of using a peer-to-peer network. They do have their purpose. But it's important to remember that these systems were designed to be like your home: safe but comfortable. A bank is a great place to keep your money and important documents, but you wouldn't want to invite your friends there to have a friendly game of cards.

Disaster Recovery

Even if you never experience an extreme level of hardware failure, you can rest assured that *some* form of failure will occur in your system at least once every two years.

Most of a PC's parts are electronic components that aren't involved in high-risk activity. They sit quietly and do their job. But wait—doesn't something in there move? Yes. The hard drive moves. It moves continuously in all but a few machines. (Those with hard drives that don't move continuously don't make good servers.) It contains platters that spin like an old record player, even when they aren't being accessed by the drive heads (which are roughly comparable to the needle on that record player). In most file server systems, the hard drive is involved in some form of activity at all times. In other words, the record is always spinning. Over the years this makes the hard drive the most vulnerable to failure.

With that in mind, what component is the most crucial to the sharing of a file server? That's right, the hard drive! Even if all of the other components in the machine fail tomorrow, if the hard drive is still intact you can place it in another system and recover your data. And data is what users value most. So, there seems to be a bit of a problem. The piece you value most is also the most likely to fail. You need a plan in case that happens.

There are many ways to skin this cat. First, look at the problem from the standpoint of what will fit your needs without breaking your bank. As usual, you can throw as much money at the problem as you like, but you need to determine how much you're really getting for your money, and how much you really need that solution (even if it is really cool to look at those extra lights in your Fort Knox MegaForce drive).

Hard Drive and Controller Schemes

One way of approaching the problem involves an idea discussed in Chapter 9—drive fault tolerance. There are many other schemes available besides the Novell approach of hard drive duplication using SFT II. (See the sections on drive mirroring and drive duplexing later in this chapter.) These schemes involve anywhere from two to an infinite number of drives, and all involve some sort of data protection through data duplication or tracking. The idea is that if one drive fails, you won't suffer a traumatic loss of critical data.

The majority of these hardware-related schemes follow an approach called RAID, for Redundant Array of Inexpensive Drives (although whether they're really inexpensive is debatable). The basic idea to avoid putting all of your eggs in one basket by spreading out the risk of failure over a number of drives. Your risk can be divided by that number of drives or less. This is sound logic. There are six levels of RAID (from 0 to 5), but this section discusses only four. Excluded are RAID level 0, which is for multiple drives only and doesn't really apply to the task at hand, and RAID level 3, which isn't a significant change from level 2 for your purposes.

RAID Level 1—Disk Drive Mirroring

Disk drive mirroring has been discussed previously as part of SFT II. It involves installing an even number of preferably identical hard disk drives into the server PC and separating the drives into two logical volumes. All data is duplicated and written to both volumes. In order for this to be effective, though, you need either hardware or software controls that enable the system to continue if a drive fails, thus tolerating the fault. If this system is running properly, the network will continue to function seamlessly (from the users' viewpoint) after a drive fails. The drives appear to be one drive to the users. This method is expensive because it requires two drives to do the work of one.

> **NOTE:**
>
> Throughout this chapter I will note whether a specific technique can be implemented with software, hardware, or both. This is significant because it can affect the performance of your file server system. If you involve software in your drive fault tolerance scheme, you demand more from your processor and memory. The primary job of a network operating system is to provide file and memory performance to the users. The alternative is to use intelligent bus mastering hard drive controllers that take control of these tasks and offload the work from the rest of the system. This will increase performance for your users.

RAID Level 2—Disk Drive Duplexing

Drive duplexing has also been discussed before as part of SFT II. It has a rather large wrinkle—there's another controller. Drive duplexing again involves installing an even number of drives (again, preferably identical) into the server PC, but this time they're attached to *two* controllers. All data is duplicated and written to each volume through its particular controller. Duplexing requires a software implementation, because you've separated the drives from the one component that could take over the task—the single hard drive controller. The biggest differences between duplexing and mirroring are the possible point of failure and the possible recovery from that failure. If the drive controller fails in a drive mirroring implementation, so do both drives, and the server will have to stop along with them. If one controller or hard drive fails in a drive duplexing implementation, however, the server continues to service the users while arrangements are made for repair.

RAID Level 4—Parity Drive Fault Tolerance (a.k.a. Data Guarding)

In order to understand RAID level 4, you must also understand the concept of parity, which goes all the way back to the concept of computer memory itself. (The plot thickens.) The idea is to have a control item that tracks what the total result should be and checks it against what the actual total result is. The control item checks for a total result that is either odd or even. Remember that computer components use 1s and 0s to communicate. So if you use a control that's looking for an odd result, and after adding the 1s and 0s the result is even, you have an error. This is an extremely simplified explanation of parity, but it would take a whole chapter to thoroughly explain it.

> **NOTE:**
>
> Intel-based machines still use memory parity today. They use eight memory chips for standard memory and one parity chip for each unit of memory. (Example: Eight 1MB memory chips and one 1MB parity chip = 1MB of RAM.) Today, for the most part, you will find all nine chips on a memory SIMM (Single In-line Memory Module) and it may appear as one unit.

In the original memory concept, the control item (a parity chip) simply returned a parity error and halted the machine completely if the bits didn't add up. Hard drive parity is more complicated than that, and rightly so. Halting the machine is of little value to you. Again, what you want is a system that tolerates faults with as little effect as possible on our users' ability to use the system. Drive parity must allow the system to continue.

RAID level 4 involves three or more drives attached to an intelligent controller that controls the fault tolerance. (See Figure 14.1.) In a system with three drives, two drives are data drives and one drive is the control (or parity) drive. The controller sends data to the drives by splitting it into equal parts and then calculating a parity algorithm based on the correct total for the data. If one of the data drives fails, the controller continues to support the users by reading the remaining data from the functioning data drives and checking it against the information on the parity drive. Then it reverses the algorithm that was arrived at earlier to produce the data. If the parity drive fails there's no effect on the data, so no algorithm is necessary.

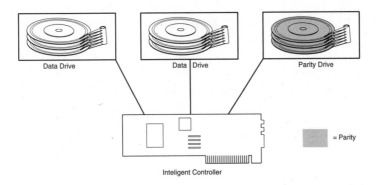

Figure 14.1.
The physical concept of RAID 4.

An analogy may help to explain this. Picture a group of people having a conversation. Let's call them Steve, Perry, and Mary. Give Perry (the parity drive) the task of tracking the total result of what is said. Steve (a data drive) says "1" and Mary (another data drive) says "0," so Perry records an odd result (1 + 0 = 1, an odd number). Suddenly, Steve gets an arrow through the heart. (The "heart drive" has crashed.) You then request the previous conversation (attempt to read the data from the drive) and find that Steve is gone. You check with Mary, who says "0," and then Perry tells you that the result should be odd. The only possible missing response, in the world of 1s and 0s, is "1."

What about drive capacity? In the first example, all three drives appear to the users as one drive, with a total capacity of all the drives but the parity drive. Three 1MB drives would yield a total capacity of 2MB (1MB data + 1MB data + 1MB parity = 2MB data). This concept is important. If there were four drives, the total capacity would be the total of three of the drives. This is a great improvement over mirroring or duplexing because you don't lose half of your drive capacity.

RAID Level 5—Distributed Parity Fault Tolerance (a.k.a. Distributed Data Guarding)

RAID level 5 is also based on drive parity, but it's now spread over a portion of all of the drives. (The plot gets downright syrupy.) In an example involving three drives, all three are data drives, and a portion of each drive contains the control or parity data. (See Figure 14.2.) The controller sends data to the drives by splitting it into equal parts and then calculating a parity algorithm based on the correct total for the data. Because data is continually written, a different drive is given the responsibility of recording the parity data. If one of the drives fails, the controller continues to support the users by reading the remaining data from the functioning drives and checking it against the parity portion of the drive that contains the parity data. Then it reverses the algorithm that was arrived at earlier to produce the data. If the parity data is located on the failed drive and all of the data can be retrieved from the remaining drives, there's no need to check parity.

The advantage of RAID 5 over RAID 4 is that parity is distributed across all of the drives, so it isn't necessary for the parity drive to be constantly busy during writes of data to the drives.

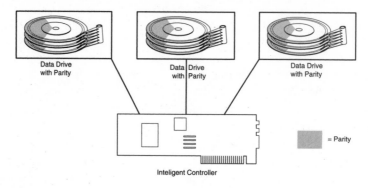

Figure 14.2.
The physical concept of RAID 4.

Back to Steve, Perry, and Mary. This time, make them take turns tracking the total result of what is said at different points in the conversation. Steve says "1" and Mary says "0," so Perry records an odd result (1 + 0 = 1, an odd number). The next time a conversation is held Perry can speak, and he says "0." Then Steve says "0," and Mary records an even result (0 + 0 = 0, an even number). Suddenly, Steve gets an arrow through the heart! (Not very lucky, that Steve fella.) You then request the previous conversation and find that Steve has fallen again. You check with Perry, who says "0," and then Mary tells you that the result should be even. The only possible missing response is 0. If Mary had been the one to get the arrow, Steve and Perry would have simply arrived at the correct result and moved on (much faster, without a thought for Mary).

This has been a brief explanation of a fairly complex concept, but it should be enough to give you a taste of this extremely useful tool. Keep in mind that what you're protecting with these schemes is shared data, most likely the biggest reason for having the network. To help you keep it all straight, the following chart gives you the possible different schemes and how they relate.

	% of Storage Lost to Fault Tolerance	*Software- or Hardware- Controlled*	*Number of Drives Necessary*	*Tolerance Method*
RAID 1	50%	Either	2 or greater even number	Drive mirroring
RAID 2	50%	Software	2 or greater even number	Drive duplexing
RAID 4	33% to 7%	Hardware	3 or more	Single parity drive pro-tecting mult-iple data drives
RAID 5	33% to 7%	Hardware	3 or more	Distributed parity across all drives

Back Up (Please!)

No matter how bulletproof your drive scheme is, no system is impervious to fail-ure. Even if you protect your drives or duplicate your file servers, you still need a way to back up and recover your data. What if there's a fire at your file server site? It's difficult to extract a hard drive from a molten pile of metal. What if your equip-ment is stolen? The thieves probably won't be kind enough to leave your data. Even if you find these ideas absurd, backing up your data is more economical than doubling the cost of your storage capacity (as you do with drive mirroring and duplexing).

There are hundreds, if not thousands, of different ways to back up your data. (If this is a new concept for you, look back at your DOS manuals or a beginner's DOS book.) Whatever backup method you choose, there are a few key issues to keep in mind.

Choose Your Weapon

Involve as few pieces of drive media as possible in the backup process. You aren't going to store the data from our server's hard drive on diskettes, obviously. The idea is to make it easier to recover the data. Also, if you need to replace media in the middle of a backup, the data is less likely to be complete when you recover it. Each new piece of media adds a new risk factor. Your goal should be to back up the entire server disk system on one piece of media.

Backup can be done on many different types of drive media. Yes, diskettes can be used, but at 1.44MB per disk, backing up the average 1-gigabyte server hard drive could take a long time. Other options include magnetic tape, digital audio tape (DAT), optical disks, and WORM drives. Of these choices, magnetic tape and DAT have been the most popular.

Magnetic tapes have been around the longest. They work (and sometimes look) much like the cassette tapes that you listen to music on. Data can be recorded on the tape and recovered later. The tape capacity ranges from 40MB to 550MB. The price range is from $200 to $1,000 per magnetic tape drive. If you have a hard drive capacity of 550MB or less, this is the most economical choice. But if you think your system is going to grow, you should consider another choice.

DAT is the second most popular choice because of the increasing size of server systems. These tapes were originally invented to record CD-quality audio. But before the manufacturers could get beyond the legalities involved with the technology, companies like Emerald had found these tapes and started selling them for use in data backup. These tapes are very dependable because of their extremely high-quality reproduction. The capacity of these drives (with the compression schemes that have been introduced) is 1 to 5 gigabytes. This capacity can be increased with auto-loading devices, which allow you to load up to 16 tapes into one magazine, increasing your capacity to 64 gigabytes. The prices range from $900 to $3,000. These systems may seem expensive if you have more than 550MB of data to store, but the convenience and reliability they offer make them well worth the money.

Optical and WORM drives are most often used to permanently archive data. The capacity of these drives is between 100MB and 2 gigabytes, so you can store a lot of data, but the discs are usually far more expensive than either magnetic tape or DAT. These devices have found a home in law firms and accounting groups that need to recover information from several years past.

Have a Plan

Make a plan and stay with it. The one time you don't back up your data will be the one time you need it. A good general rule is to be no farther away from your previous backup than the amount of work you would like to repeat. So if you don't mind repeating a week's worth of data entry, back up just once a week. Then again, backing up every fifteen minutes isn't efficient either. Normal backup schemes call for a backup every night of the workweek.

There are three types of backups:

* ✖ The first is the most obvious—full backup. Back up all of the data on every drive in your server.

* ✖ The second is incremental backup. Back up only the data that has been changed since your last backup of any kind. You use less tape because you aren't backing up files that you've already backed up.

* ✖ The third is differential backup. Back up all of the data that has been changed since your last *full* backup. This is different than incremental backup, because you back up data that has already been backed up, all the way back to the last full backup. This makes restoration easier because you have just two tapes to refer to at any given time, but as the days progress it takes more tape to do the backup.

Your backup plan itself can involve any of these methods, but you also need to include the frequency of backups. There are many different schemes for how often to back up data, but the one that has stood the test of time and is simplest to understand is the Grandfather, Father, Son method. (The name comes from the chronological relationship between the tapes.)

The scheme involves five tapes the first week, and one tape for each successive week after that for four weeks. It can be extrapolated to give you data recovery as far back as you like. To begin, mark your first five tapes with the names of the days of the week. Start on Monday with a full backup on the tape marked *Monday.* On Tuesday, Wednesday, and Thursday, perform either a full, incremental, or differential backup (your choice, based on the previously mentioned facts) on each of the respective tapes. On Friday, do another full backup, and take that Friday tape off-site to protect it from physical damage (fire, theft, etc.). Start the process again the next week, but from then on you need only do an incremental or differential backup on Mondays if you've chosen to use that method. On Friday, add a new *Friday* tape, do a full backup, and take the tape off-site. Continue this process every week, replacing the *Friday* tapes and taking them off-site. You can start recycling the *Friday* tapes after the fourth Friday if you like. This scheme enables you to recover any data changed in the last month.

With this plan, you can recover data written to your drives as far back as you like by removing, storing, and replacing a tape at any time during the process. Companies often keep one tape for each month so they can return to a version of a file that existed during that timeframe. If the books won't balance in August, the problem may be related to a mistake that happened months before. Going back to those previous tapes and recovering the information from when everything was okay can be a real lifesaver.

389

Here's one other thing to consider: Do you want your backup device to be on your server or on a workstation? There are two schools of thought on this idea. If you put your backup device on a workstation, your data is protected from physical disasters that can destroy your server. In the rare case that the server and the newly backed-up tape from the workstation are destroyed, you lose the new data that was backed up. However, you depend on the network protocol and topology to deliver that data when you want to recover it. This is slow and risky. Workstation backups also usually require the user to properly configure the workstation for the backup.

Server-based backups don't require a user to be responsible for setting up a proper backup environment. Also, the data gets to the backup device quicker. It's best if a backup device that's connected directly to the server is put on a separate controller from the hard drive. That way it can use the full controller channel to obtain or distribute the data.

Depend on human intervention as little as possible in the backup process. People will forget a step or run out of time, leaving your backup undone. Today's software packages can run a backup unattended, and can retain a catalog of files that have been backed up for quicker recovery. There's another good reason for putting the backup unit on the file server; the backup will get done even if the users forget to replace the tape.

Server Redundancy

Server redundancy is the closest thing to a bulletproof vest that you can get in networking technology. It involves connecting two file servers with a high-speed dedicated network segment and maintaining the same data on both servers. If the primary server encounters any hardware failures, the other server takes over until repairs can be made.

Novell is the only company in the PC networking industry that currently supports this type of redundancy. Novell's product is NetWare SFT level III. It's very expensive; you're paying for twice the amount of hardware and an extra network cabling segment. However, some networks have mission-critical systems that can't afford to be lost. If this is your situation, carefully plan your steps and be sure that your servers are exact duplicates.

Power Protection

The most common cause of hardware failure is erratic power delivery. Power surges and dips can throw an otherwise stable environment into chaos. Keep in mind that most server platforms don't immediately write the data delivered to them on the physical drive. They hold the data in memory and allow the user to go on his merry way. Then they write the data during times of low user demand. If your server loses power when your critical data is in memory and not on a physical drive, you're in big trouble. Not only that, but a good deal of the time your server operating system is in danger of being corrupted.

The solution to this problem is to provide your server with some type of power protection. The best device for this kind of protection is an *uninterruptible power supply (UPS)*. This is also called a battery backup because it contains a large battery that maintains power. A UPS keeps your server system running if power fails, and the good units provide power conditioning as well. Power conditioning is important, because two of the few things that can destroy the solid-state electronics in your server are noise and fluctuations in the correct amount of power.

Something else to consider in this plan is whether or not the UPS will communicate with your server. The better UPSs send a signal to your server if the power fails and allow the server to come down in an orderly fashion. This is important, because even if the UPS is capable of carrying a system for 20 or 30 minutes, often the power drops and comes back up more than once in a short span of time. This up-and-down power can drain the battery, and before long your system can go unprotected.

Error Correcting Code (ECC) Memory

Error correcting memory has been around for years in the mainframe and mini-computer world, but it has only recently made its appearance in PC-based server systems. Simply put, ECC is a memory scheme that allows for memory redundancy that's loosely like that found in drive redundancy. High-speed memory takes over if a failure occurs, and the users aren't affected. This is important because if the memory in your server finds a parity error, it has no choice but to shut the system down completely and immediately. This could be fatal.

Disaster Recovery Summary

There are many things to consider when it comes to disaster recovery, but the one thing you should remember from this chapter is the importance of having a plan. It does no good to have the equipment if you don't use it. Even if you have a duplicated file server with mirrored RAID 5 server volumes (and obviously more money than you know what to do with), you're still susceptible to site disasters and software corruption. So back up regularly.

Keep your disaster recovery plan reasonable. You can spend as much money as you like, but that may not always be the smartest plan. More important than how much something costs is how reputable the hardware vendor is when it comes to quality and support. The last thing you want to encounter when your server has failed is a support line that's only open from 1 to 4 p.m. on Monday, Wednesday, and Friday. Server components don't fail on schedule.

What Have You Learned?

1. Even usernames can be something to consider when you're looking at server security.

2. Password security has many different variables. If you make it too complicated, it can become a hindrance instead of a help.

3. Once the user logs into the system, there are many different combinations of rights and attributes that control where she can go and what is available to her.

4. The hard drive is at the same time the most necessary shared peripheral and the most likely to fail because of its moving parts.

5. Hard drives need not be left to die alone. There are many different implementations for hard drive installation that enable you to recover from a failure without affecting user access.

6. Tape backup is important even if you have a solid fault tolerance method in place for hard drives.

7. Corrupted data doesn't usually present itself until many days after the corruption occurs. Therefore, backing up your data is done for reasons other than tolerating drive failure. It also enables you to recover uncorrupted data from previous versions found on tape. You don't need to do a full backup every time, and doing so may not be the easiest or most economical choice. Plan your backups, and follow a schedule to be sure that you're always safe.

8. Power protection is a very important part of any disaster recovery scheme.

9. ECC memory can prevent memory parity errors from shutting down your system.

The Future of Networking 15

1. Which computing services have traditionally served the strategic needs of organizations, and which have served tactical needs?

2. What is missing from many companies' forays into network solutions that explains why their networks aren't a success?

3. What is a better term than *peer-to-peer networking*, and why?

4. What are the "new mainframes"?

5. What are the current needs for file servers and IPN systems?

6. What can you expect from the networks of the future?

7. What should you look out for as the networking market develops?

Where Are We?

The state of networking today is rich, complex, and, on the whole, highly confusing. The demands of sophisticated services, high-speed connections, global directory services, network management facilities, and robust fault tolerance are becoming real commercial issues rather than hovering on the bleeding edge of technology, as they did a couple of years ago. They're becoming strategic issues, rather than the tactical issues they were, because the world is changing. In Chapter 1 you learned how LANs came about and why they've become important to business. But to understand the big picture, you need to understand how the business environment itself has changed.

> **NOTE:**
>
> Just to make sure we're all on the same wavelength, perhaps I should distinguish between strategy and tactics.
>
> Tactics are short-term (anything up to a couple of years) steps that are carefully worked out to achieve a purpose. Strategies, on the other hand, are long-term (usually three to five years in business), large-scale plans that lead to a major goal or objective. To execute a strategy (for example, world domination), you need to define a number of tactics (for example, raising an army, training them, and so on).
>
> The distinction between the two is subtle but important. Many people focus on tactics and lose sight of strategy, while others forget that tactics are a part of the strategy. In the latter case, these people's plans look less like strategies and more like collections of tactics flying loosely in formation.
>
> Another distinction that people are often confused about is the difference between involvement and commitment. A company that's *involved* in networking is taking the tactical approach and looking for short-term benefits. On the other hand, a business that's *committed* to networking is taking a strategic role, ensuring that networking is central to the way they conduct business now and in the future.
>
> By way of analogy, have you ever had bacon and eggs for breakfast? It's a wonderful example of the distinction between involvement and commitment—the chicken was involved, but the pig was committed.

The information age that's so often talked about is only just beginning. The fact that computing is almost 50 years old doesn't mean we're out of the diapers stage yet. (Yeah, I know you could argue that it's a lot older than that, but this is my book, so...)

For example, the biggest challenge for many network managers is simply keeping the network running! This is because most networks have grown tactically. "Oh, we need to connect accounts," they said back in 1980-something. "Engineering needs to share documents," they said soon after. "Why don't we put sales on-line?" was then heard. Soon, every department had at least one network. "Ah!" they finally said, "We should join these all up and get a network manager."

Lo and behold, they did join them up, and they got a huge network made up of tons of stuff, and they hired a network manager who soon found out that he didn't have a clue what those tons of stuff actually consisted of. I've talked to network managers who cheerfully (or sheepishly) admit that they have no idea of what is really out there and whether it works right. (I think their attitude depends on how much of the mess they created.)

What makes this critical is that, with the recent trend of downsizing, our networks have become the focus of our computing resources. They are increasingly critical to conducting business and therefore to the success of that business. In short, they are becoming a strategic business weapon that's as crucial to business success as having telephones, and occasionally more valuable than the staff that operates them!

The reason for this centrality is that as networks become the corporate nervous system, they come to embody the intelligence of the organization. When the network fails, the organization may be effectively dead as well. The problem becomes, "No network services, no access to databases. No access to databases, no order-taking, because committing to delivery isn't possible when we can't see the stock records. No order-taking, no clients."

The latest market pull is for companies to start doing business on the greatest network in the world—the Internet. The reason is the sheer size of the Internet population, estimated in June 1994 to be 3.2 million computers on more than 25,000 networks, servicing some 25 million people per day. Some pundits estimate that the Internet will service one billion people worldwide by the year 2000.

They won't just be computer-literate people. They'll be home users, small businesses, and school kids. They'll be doctors, lawyers, you name it. And the Internet won't be brought to them by PCs only. It will come to a large number of people through television-mediated services, through the cable companies and new, sophisticated cable signal converter units. You'll see text, graphics, animations, and computer data overlaid on regular television pictures, and you'll be able to interact with the computers that supply the data.

The opportunities already being discussed for home shopping, home banking, and a whole range of consumer information services are enough to make Wall Street start breathing very heavily.

With this kind of audience and business potential, opportunities are in sight to close the loop, to remove expensive and potentially error-laden human interaction from the process of fulfilling a customer order.

For example, it's the year 2000 and a consumer in Edinburgh, Scotland, is sitting at home thinking, "Ah, winter's coming and I need a new coat." (It does indeed get mighty cold up there.) He selects the shopping channel and checks the index to see who has three-quarter-length wool coats available. He then selects a price range and views video clips of the various styles in that range being worn (much better than just looking at a still picture). He decides that he likes model 25E in medium from Hang Sun Coats in Hong Kong and places his order.

HSC takes the order and verifies the client's credit card details (supplied with the order) with the credit card company in London. Then the client's measurements are retrieved from his cable signal converter (I told you the box was smart), the transaction details and sizing are confirmed with him, and the order is sent to the factory.

At the factory, a warehouse retrieves the cloth, computer-controlled robots cut the material, and robot sewing machines join the pieces. Another robot wraps and boxes the finished goods and packs the box on the next shipment to Scotland. The first human to make contact with the box is the postman (assuming the postal service still exists).

Throughout this whole scenario are networks. Networks transport the data from the video servers in the cable office to the consumer. They transfer the order from the consumer to the vendor, the credit enquiry from the vendor to the credit bureau, and the data from the order-taking system to the robot manufacturing system. The manufacturing system is networked to the accounting system, the goods ordering system, and the warehouse system (which might not even be the manufacturer's warehouse!). The shipping instructions are sent from the vendor's computers to the shipper's computer, and so on.

And that little glimpse into the future is only the tip of the iceberg (or should that be infoberg?).

The future of Western civilization is now so predicated upon computer-mediated communications—that is, networks—that it's inconceivable that our economies could function without them.

The Hierarchy

Companies have built a computing hierarchy. (See Figure 15.1.) At the bottom are the PCs, which are there to enhance and support personal productivity—essentially, they're the tactical tools for getting business done. At the top are the corporate mainframes, which serve the long-term strategic goals of the company. Just below and sometimes beside the mainframes are the minicomputers, which service departments or business units.

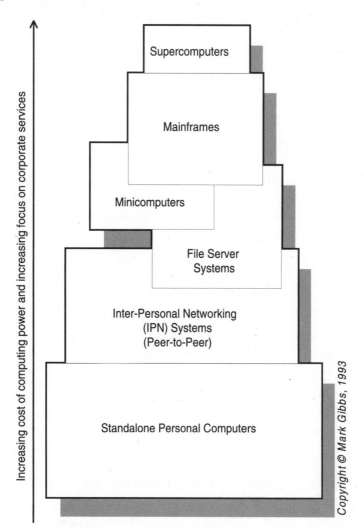

Figure 15.1.
The computing hierarchy.

399

Sitting in the middle, currently both below and alongside the minicomputers, are the file servers, which are used mainly in a departmental role. But with the drive for rightsizing, they're becoming corporate-level resources, vying with the main-frames in a surprising number of areas. Indeed, the use of groupware, workflow systems, and services like LAN-based electronic mail have made networks the nervous systems of some organizations, leaving mainframes and minis to do what they're really good at—processing data.

The owners of the file server systems, either management information services (MIS) or a particular department, are pretty happy with this arrangement as it stands. Not only have they expanded the scope of computing in the organization by distributing the processing, but they've managed to maintain control of the resources through centralization.

Interpersonal Networking

Right behind the file server systems are the young turks of the networking busi-ness: the peer-to-peer networks. Although we blithely use the term *peer-to-peer*, it has become woefully inadequate to express the capabilities of these systems. I'd like to replace it with the term *interpersonal networking (IPN)*, which defines the reality of what users want to do: network on a personal level.

The importance of this want is partially due to the limitations of PC environments. In front of a user, on a desk, is a PC. This PC both has and needs resources (unless its user is very rich or is at a high level in the company). To get the job done, the PC owner needs to get data from other people, pass data to them to work with and return, and use available resources.

When the resources are centered at the server, the path of communications is ef-fectively up and down the organization's computing hierarchy. Although this can be made to work, in general it doesn't. The tools simply aren't there unless the company makes a big, bold commitment.

An example of making this type of commitment is implementing Lotus Notes. This is not a trivial undertaking, by any stretch of the imagination, if there are more than a few people to get up and running. Notes takes planning, training, development, and management if the organization is to see a quantifiable benefit. Even then, the company needs a commitment from the top down to making the plan strategic and beneficial.

Basic multi-user services like e-mail that would seem to be pretty straightforward often don't really become a core company service, even if the company has imple-mented the system organization-wide. Why? Because the company isn't committed.

A common situation is for the senior management to be gung ho about the service but then continue to issue memos on paper at the rate of a small forest every week.

When groups of users need tools to make them more productive, what they often wind up with is a corporate system that is barely adequate. The company thought it was installing a silk purse, and what it gave the users was a sow's ear.

Now coming onto the scene are interpersonal networking products that cost little more than a decent video adapter card or an office chair. A department or workgroup can subversively introduce IPN technology, and before you know it there are all sorts of workgroups and cooperative projects and information exchanges. There are also hundreds of new threats to security and integrity, but only MIS cares. Indeed, MIS folks are generally less than enthusiastic about IPN products because they're essentially anarchists.

Unfortunately for MIS, it's already too late to do anything about the influx of IPS services. Unless the company can put real, compelling force behind the MIS dictates, IPN systems are there to stay.

The Risks

So what's at risk? Well, data integrity and security are pretty high on the list. With all that data being easily moved about, the rather weak security offered by most IPN systems (LANtastic is the exception), and users' customary failure to use the security services, often anyone on the network can go data surfing anywhere.

Another issue to consider is that computer viruses, hackers, and espionage become serious menaces in these kinds of loose environments. The lack of access controls and the flexibility of IPN systems means that, for example, viruses have many more paths between the PCs. So even if the organization uses antivirus tools, it's likely to find that infections, once they start, are pernicious unless the PCs using IPN services are engineered to meet acceptable reliability and integrity standards.

A Turning Point

In summary, we're at a turning point in networking. (See Figure 15.2.) File server systems have become the central network data stores (replacing mainframes) and are evolving into the engines for supporting communications on an enterprise-wide basis. File servers also provide horizontal connectivity at the interdepartmental and interworkgroup levels.

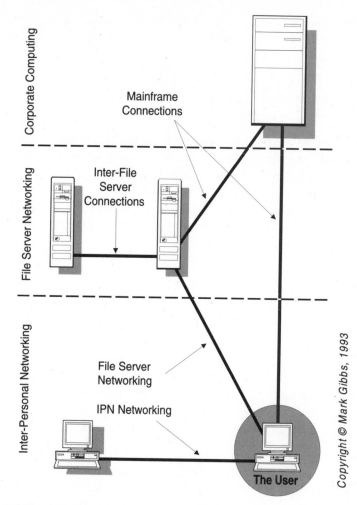

Figure 15.2.
The network connectivity hierarchy.

IPN products are ideal tools for integrating users into workgroups and creating personal, horizontal connectivity in the local area. And with Microsoft and Novell making major pushes into the IPN market, the technologies are becoming acceptable to people who would have dismissed them as toys a year or so ago.

Current Needs for File Server Systems

There is one certainty when it comes to computers: they're never powerful enough. The system that makes you say "Wow!" today will look weak and underpowered tomorrow. And power is about more than just raw performance, how fast the processor and disk run. It's also about how much RAM the computer can use, how big its disk storage system can be, how fast it can communicate over a network, and how many transactions per second it can perform. Here are the critical areas:

- **More performance.** As the rightsizing trend continues, servers are expected to offer more functionality (communications services, management services, and so on), more RAM (16MB per server is not unusual at the moment), more disk capacity (a gigabyte per server is becoming common), and faster processors (Intel Pentium 100MHz microprocessors are the current proven technology at the top end).
- **Greater reliability.** As servers get bigger and faster, they also have a far greater impact when they fail. Redundant disk subsystems (mirroring and duplexing) are a good first step, and redundant file servers (as found with NetWare SFT III) are mandatory components for achieving better reliability. More distributed services are also needed—services that may not be file server-based, but that have the same kinds of robustness. If I'm disconnected from a server and its redundant companion, why should I be cut off from electronic messaging services or printing services? Also, the kind of redundancy in the distributed directory services discussed under VINES and NetWare 4 is needed for all data services. Although some of these goals can be achieved, at present they have to be custom-built, and they often don't integrate well with existing management tools.
- **Greater manageability.** File server system design has progressed at a breakneck speed since the mid-eighties, and these systems have become far more manageable. Much still needs to be done, however, to make multiple file server systems and all of their associated network services manageable as a single unit. Currently, you might easily need a dozen separate tools that use six different user interfaces to manage your network. Even more irritating and difficult is trying to combine information from the different tools to analyze performance or diagnose problems. The tools usually aren't designed to work with each other.

- **Better user interfaces.** To access file server services, users currently need to know a fair amount about the system. Although it's possible to train users to be more effective, the systems of the future will offer stronger and more robust user interfaces to let the user concentrate on the job rather than on the network.

Current Needs for Peer-to-Peer Network Systems

With IPN systems becoming a business trend rather than being seen as a toy, questions about how and where they can be used are starting to be examined. Although performance is on the list of critical issues where peer-to-peer systems need improvement, there are other areas that are perhaps even more critical.

- **Performance.** IPN systems are improving in this area, and Artisoft's LANtastic is a good example. It now boasts performance that rivals NetWare 3.x at the 20-user level. But performance is not just about input/output speed (although it is of fundamental importance). It's also concerned with the number of connections from clients to servers, the number of clients per server, and so on. In these areas, IPN systems are still more limited than many organizations would like.
- **Robustness.** As IPN systems become more complex (supporting Windows, gateways to other systems, and so on), they start to show their rough edges. This results in unreliability and crashes, neither of which are acceptable in a workgroup environment (or any PC environment, for that matter). IPN systems need to become far more robust if they are to really become part of business computing.
- **Manageability.** IPN systems are anarchic in much the same way that early PCs and LANs were. They can be introduced into groups and departments alongside existing network systems for such a low price that official sanction isn't sought. But because IPN systems are weak in security, they're also weak in manageability. Data can wander around freely in IPN systems, and controlling who gets what is a nightmare if the IPN system has a lot of users (say, more than 20). What's needed are comprehensive management systems that let someone who will effectively be an IPN network manager take control of the whole IPN system.

> **NOTE:**
> Once IPN systems are installed and in use, you'll never get rid of them without a real political battle. You'll have to deal with the fact that the IPN systems are probably making people more productive, or at least making their work easier. If you take the IPN systems away, you'd better have a good replacement to fill the gap.

✖ **Security.** With the exception of a couple of products (LANtastic, for example), IPN systems have extremely weak security. The current assumption by many vendors is that security gets in the way of using IPN systems. In any environment where money and business are involved, this is like saying that traffic lights get in the way of driving. Sure they do, but they prevent accidents and regulate activity. Computer systems need security if they're going to be useful in the long term. Without security, PCs become tactical solutions that in the long term may cost you money rather than making or saving money.

The Future: The Author's Gigawatt Crystal Ball Swings into Action

What can you expect of networking in the next few years?

✖ **Networks everywhere:** At present, around 50 percent of corporate PCs are networked. Within the next decade, you can expect to see this rise to 80 percent or more. Some of the new wireless technologies will make electronic messaging an integral part of almost any machine, so even though a PC may not be on a high-speed network, it can still be networked. It will then be able to use groupware services, such as calendaring and workflow that's mediated by electronic messaging. In short, you won't be able to escape networking. Even simple devices such as photocopiers and security systems will be integrated into networks. (Printers are already coming with built-in network interfaces.)

✖ **Electronic messaging everywhere:** The number of electronic mailboxes is growing exponentially, and in the next decade you'll see an explosion of PC-based messaging services that will make most businesspeople in the Western hemisphere available by e-mail. Already the telephone companies are introducing publicly available e-mail systems that can translate between different message formats. Global public e-mail directory services will be available, and you'll be able to find people (those who want to be found) anywhere in the world.

✖ **Faster everything:** Network transports will get faster, PCs will get faster, disk storage will get faster, and you'll still think it's all running far too slow as operating systems such as Windows NT, Taligent's Pink, and other even more exotic new operating system products soak up performance on the desktop.

✖ **Faster networks:** Along with the new operating systems will be the need to move greater quantities of data, because the operating systems and their applications will be built to do more complex things. This is already happening; consider the explosion of multimedia products that use megabytes of data per second. Transport performance will be affected, network interface adapter cards will be pushed to their limits, and so on. Already, 100 Mbit/s technologies are not unusual for backbone systems that interconnect several networks. Within a decade, the top-end performance could easily be on the order of tens of gigabits (thousands of megabits) per second for local area connections, and today's LAN speeds will be available over regional and possibly national areas.

✖ **IPN everywhere:** IPN services will be standard parts of desktop operating systems. This is already the case with Macintosh System 7, and is promised with Windows NT. Novell is threatening to make IPN an embedded service (that is, an integral part of the network operating system) for NetWare 4 clients, and a variety of other systems are on the way. In the next decade, IPN technologies will mature and become as commonplace as file server-based networks are today.

✖ **Global directories everywhere:** Global directory services will become standard network technology for both file server systems (this is already happening) and IPN systems (Novell had a shot at it with NetWare Lite). The interaction between the real objects and their representations in the global directories will become more active, and workflow and scheduling services may well become an integral part of directory services.

✖ **Distributed computing services:** The concept of network computing will solidify, and services will emerge that enable applications to use spare computing power on other PCs. For example, if you're doing a complex simulation of a road system or a production process that involves thousands of variables, you might want to distribute the processing of certain parts of the model to other resources so you can get results quickly.

✖ **Lots of jobs:** People who understand networks will be in demand, and experience with networking will be an important part of your resume.

✖ **Internet connections everywhere:** Within five years, not having an e-mail address that's reachable through the Internet will mean that you're a hermit, a monk, a prisoner (although don't be surprised if they decide that an e-mail address is every inmate's right), or not in business. Your LANs will be connected to the Internet, and you'll use Internet resources transparently (wherever they are, even on the other side of the country or the world).

✖ And most importantly, %&*^%^%&)*^&*^

Damn! Blew a fuse on the crystal ball. Guess you'll just have to wait and see what else comes along. Even without the crystal ball, I can tell you that, for those people who can get involved and capitalize on the growth of the networking market, it's going to be exciting and probably a lot of fun.

What Have You Learned?

1. Traditionally, the strategic needs of an organization have been served by mainframe systems, and the tactical needs have been served by personal computers. Networking is making it possible to turn PCs into a strategic force in an organization at significantly less cost than a mainframe.

2. Many companies don't make a real commitment to making network systems pay off. Without support from the board downward, it's hard to build a philosophy of use that makes network solutions a real payback.

3. Interpersonal networking, or IPN, is a better term than peer-to-peer networking because it describes why these systems are used—to connect people to other people, rather than to services.

4. File server systems are "the new mainframes," because the services they offer are centralized and only the processing is distributed.

5. For file servers, the current needs are more performance, greater reliability, better management, and better user interfaces. For IPN systems, the needs are greater robustness, better performance, and better security.

6. Networks of the future will be everywhere, and electronic messaging will be available to the majority of PC users. There will be a general speeding up of all services (particularly network transports). Interpersonal networking will become a ubiquitous service, global directories will be available in all systems that interconnect, there'll be a rise of distributed computing services, and there'll be an almost endless job market for people with networking expertise.

7. As the networking market develops, you should look out for fun, excitement, and my next book.

A

Where to Next?

If learning about networks has inspired you or even just caught your interest, you'll probably want to go on and find out more. There was a time when trying to find out about networks was difficult. Today, the problem is quite the opposite! To help you through this quagmire of data (remember, it's not information until it has meaning and purpose for you), the following resources are, on the whole, invaluable.

> **NOTE:**
>
> The expression "straight from the horse's mouth" goes back to when horse traders wouldn't accept a seller's word about the age of a horse. (They still won't, for that matter.) Instead, they looked in the beast's mouth for confirmation. Networking and etymology all in one book—what a value!

Books

There are now vast numbers of books on various networking topics, but most are pretty useless for the beginning networker. However, I hope that you will find some of the following titles useful:

Computer Networks, Second Edition
Andrew S. Tannenbaum, 1989
Publisher: Prentice Hall International Editions
ISBN: 0-13-166836-6

An excellent book that gets very technical, but in a clear, well-structured way. Tannenbaum is one of the best writers of textbook-type material about computers. If you're getting deeper into networking, this is one that you'll find really useful.

Do-It-Yourself Networking with LANtastic
Mark Gibbs, 1992
Publisher: Sams Publishing
ISBN: 0-672-30026-5

Although some might consider it a little tacky for me to cite my own work, I don't care. This book focuses on LANtastic, but the discussion of planning and designing a LAN is relevant to anyone looking into the topic of networking. This is also a great present for friends, loved ones, children, and so on.

Absolute Beginner's Guide to Programming
Greg Perry, 1993
Publisher: Sams Publishing
ISBN: 0-672-30269-1

If you're doing anything that involves programming on networks, and programming is something you haven't come to grips with, you need this excellent introduction.

Distributed Systems and Computer Networks
Morris Sloman and Jeff Kramer, 1987
Publisher: Prentice Hall
ISBN: 0-13-215864-3

A useful textbook that goes deeply into protocol and architecture issues and discusses the details of network communications design.

Periodicals

The last couple of years have seen an explosion of magazines and newsletters that cover networking. The following is my list of highly recommended periodicals:

LAN Computing	(215) 957-4269
LAN Magazine	(800) 234-9573
LAN Technology	(800) 456-1654
LAN Times	(415) 513-6800
Network World	(800) 622-1108

Many of the general computing magazines now cover networking:

Computerworld	(800) 669-1002
MacWEEK	(609) 461-2100
PC Week	(617) 350-7035
Byte Magazine	(800) 232-2983
PC Magazine	(800) 289-0429
PC Computing	(800) 365-2770
Corporate Computing	(800) 688-1451

Information Services

You can read until your eyes cross, but if you don't make contact with the experts and other users, you're just out in the weeds. You should plan to get online or join user groups.

CompuServe

Of all of the resources, CompuServe is a must. After books, CompuServe is the best way to keep up to date with networking and get answers to almost any technical question. If you haven't used CompuServe before, it's a sort of bulletin board system of phenomenal proportions. It has forums for just about everything, from avocado farming to zoology, and tens of thousands of files to download.

Want to know what the options are for connecting to an obscure minicomputer? If the information isn't in a file that you can download, it can be found on a forum. Often you'll get a reply within 24 hours, although I've had replies come back in 10 minutes!

Just to give you an idea of how much networking information is available on CompuServe, the following list contains some of the forums that you can join:

Artisoft Forum	ARTISOFT
Banyan Forum	BANFORUM
Client Server Computing Forum	MSNETWORKS
IBM Communications Forum	IBMCOM
Lan Magazine Forum	LANMAG
Lan Technology Forum	LANTECH
Macintosh Systems Forum	MACSYS
National Computer Security Association	NCSA
Novell Forum A	NOVA
Novell Forum B	NOVB
Novell Forum C	NOVC
Novell Forum D	NOVD
Novell Library Forum	NOVLIB
Novell NetWire	NOVELL
Novell Vendor Forum	NOVVEN
PC Vendor B Forum	PCVENB
PC Vendor D Forum	PCVEND
PC Vendor E Forum	PCVENE
PC Vendor F Forum	PCVENF

Support On Site	ONSITE
Telecommunications Forum	TELECOM
Thomas-Conrad Forum	TCCFORUM

For more information or to join, call CompuServe at (800) 848-8990. You can also join online by setting your modem to 300, 1,200, 2,400, or 9,600 bits per second, with seven data bits, even parity, one stop bit, and full duplex. To find the CompuServe access number nearest you, dial (800) 346-3247. When the CompuServe modem answers, press Enter. When you see the prompt Host Name, type PHONES and follow the menus. When you have the number of the nearest CompuServe node, use it, press Enter, and follow the menus. When you get online, send a message to [75600,1002] and let me know what you're doing with networks.

User Groups

User groups are terrific organizations, particularly when they're well supported by the vendor. You'll find other people who are wrestling with the same problems as you. Most of the groups have newsletters, and the regular meetings often feature speakers from the vendor or third-party suppliers.

NetWare Users International (NUI)

You'll probably find a NetWare user group fairly near to you (unless you live up on a mountain in Bolivia). These groups (about 300 worldwide, with 140,000 members) are well supported by users and Novell, and you can get onto Novell's mailing list if you join. (In the course of a year you can receive a small deciduous forest in easy-to-handle chunks through the mail.) Members get a monthly newsletter, and NUI organizes NetWare user conferences in many locations. (These are user-driven events and are always worth attending.) For further information on NUI, contact:

NetWare Users International
P.O. Box 19007
Provo, UT 84605
Telephone: (800) 228-4684/(801) 429-7177
Fax: (801) 429-3056

413

NOTE:

It's a source of amazement to me that most of these companies still want to send out paper! Wouldn't it be nice if they sent you whatever data they wanted to bombard you with on disk, and then offered it to you on paper if you requested it? On the same soapbox, check out how few computer companies can be contacted through electronic mail. Sure, certain people in each organization can be contacted, but most (usually the people you really want to contact) are still available by snail mail and the telephone only. (*Snail mail* is a derogatory term used by the electronic mail industry and users to describe the regular mail service. Having just had some mail disappear between the sender and me, I'd say the snail is hungry as well as slow.)

Association of Banyan Users International (ABUI)

The ABUI is managed by Smith, Bucklin, and Associates. Call (312) 644-6610 and ask for the ABUI Coordinator. This will get you on the mailing list for the bimonthly *NetWork News* magazine. (I just got the latest issue and it's very good.) There are around 30 ABUI groups in the U.S. and several in Europe. ABUI also holds conferences in the U.S. several times a year.

LANtastic User Groups

These are relatively new organizations. (There are about 25 of them in the U.S.) As far as I know, they don't call themselves LUGs, but that's probably just as well. For more information and details about a LANtastic User Group near you, call Artisoft Sales at (800) TINYRAM or (602) 293-4000.

Vendors

Most of the following vendors produce huge quantities of printed materials, which they will send you for free. Some of it is really useful. You'll find lots of helpful information in what the industry calls *white papers* (documents that explain a vendor's position on a topic). These usually give you background on that topic, so they can be invaluable. Many vendors also produce primers on their products and the product technologies. Many also hold seminars that end-users can attend. (Sometimes they even supply coffee and doughnuts.)

ACCTON Technology
46750 Fremont Boulevard
Suite 104
Fremont, CA 94538
Telephone: (415) 226-9800

Action Technologies
2200 Powell Street
11th Floor
Emeryville, CA 94608
Telephone: (800) 624-2162

Apple Computer
20525 Mariani Avenue
Cupertino, CA 95014
Telephone: (408) 996-1010

Artisoft, Inc.
691 E. River Rd.
Tucson, AZ 85704
Telephone: (800) TINYRAM/(602) 293-4000
Fax: (602) 293-8065

Banyan Systems, Inc.
120 Flanders Road
Westboro, MA 01581
Telephone: (800) 828-2404 or 828-5332/(508) 898-1000
Fax: (508) 898-1755

Beyond, Inc.
38 Sidney Street
Cambridge, MA 02139
Telephone: (617) 621-0095
Fax: (617) 621-0096

Borland International
1800 Green Falls Road
P.O. Box 660001
Scotts Valley, CA 95067-0001
Telephone: (800) 331-0877/(408) 438-8400
Fax: (408) 439-9272

CBIS
5875 Peachtree Industrial Boulevard
Building 100, Unit 170
Norcross, GA 30092
Telephone: (404) 446-1332

Cheyenne Software, Inc.
55 Bryant Avenue
Roslyn, NY 11576-9850
Telephone: (800) 243-9462/(516) 484-5110
Fax: (516) 484-3446

Coactive Computing Corporation
1301 Shoreway Road
Suite 221
Belmont, CA 94002
Telephone: (415) 802-1080
Fax: (415) 593-9304

Compex
4055 East La Palma Avenue
Suite C
Anaheim, CA 92807
Telephone: (714) 630-7302

DaVinci Systems
P.O. Box 17449
Raleigh, NC 27619
Telephone: (800) 326-3556

Digital Communications Associates, Inc. (DCA)
1000 Alderman Drive
Alpharetta, GA 30202-4199
Telephone: (800) 348-3221/(404) 442-4000
Fax: (404) 442-4366

DSC Communications Corp.
1000 Coit Road
Plano, TX 75075
Telephone: (800) 322-3101/(214) 519-3000

Futurus, Inc.
3131 North I-10 Service Road
Suite 401
Metairie, LA 70002
Telephone: (800) 327-8296/(504) 837-1554
Fax: (504) 837-3429

Grapevine LAN Products
15323 Northeast 90th Street
Redmond, WA 98052
Telephone: (206) 869-2707

David Harris
Pegasus Mail
P.O. Box 5451
Dunedin, New Zealand

Hayes Microcomputer Products
P.O. Box 105203
Atlanta, GA 30348
Telephone: (404) 441-1617

IBM
Old Orchard Road
Armonk, NY 10504
Telephone: (800) 426-2468

Invisible Software
1165 Chess Drive
Suite D
Foster City, CA 94404
Telephone: (415) 570-5967

LanMark
P.O. Box 246
Postal Station A
Mississauga, Ontario, Canada L5A 3G8
Telephone: (416) 848-6865

Lotus Development Corporation
55 Cambridge Parkway
Cambridge, MA 02142
Telephone: (617) 577-8500
Fax: (617) 693-4663

Microsoft Corporation
One Microsoft Way
Redmond, WA 98052
Telephone: (800) 426-9400

Notework Corporation
72 Kent Street
Brookline, MA 02146
Telephone: (617) 734-4317

Novell, Inc.
122 East 1700 South
Provo, UT 84606-6194
Telephone: (800) 453-1267/(801) 429-7000
Fax: (801) 429-5775

Performance Technology
7800 IH 10, West
800 Lincoln Center
San Antonio, TX 78230
Telephone: (800) 327-8526/(512) 524-0500 or 524-2000

PowerCore, Inc.
1 Diversatech Drive
Manteno, IL 60950
Telephone: (800) 237-4754/(815) 468-3737
Fax: (815) 468-3867

Sitka Corporation
950 Marina Village Parkway
Alameda, CA 94501
Telephone: (800) 445-8677/(415) 769-9669
Fax: (415) 769-8771

Thomas-Conrad Corporation
1908-R Kramer Lane
Austin, TX 78758
Telephone: (800) 332-8683/(512) 836-1935
Fax: (512) 836-2840

WordPerfect Corporation
1555 North Technology Way
Orem, UT 84057
Telephone: (800) 321-4566

Problem Solving (Or, How to Make Technical Support Really Like You)

Whether you belong to an organization's support group, use a dealer or systems integrator, or rely on manufacturers to give you support, you can make your life, and everyone else's, a lot easier by following a few simple procedures. The objective is to solve as many problems as you can by yourself. When you can't find a solution or the problem is outside of your experience, following the approach discussed here will help you understand the scope of the problem. Then, when you have to go to the support people, you'll have the information they need. If you make their life easier, the quality of the service you get will improve.

A Few Rules

There are a few simple rules that will simplify your presentation of problems to technical support.

Rule 1: Know the System

There's no one harder to work with than a user who has a problem but can't explain it, and who doesn't really know the equipment or software. For example, if you've got a problem with your networked PC but you don't know what network operating system you're running, don't expect to communicate well with the technical support people. A good ploy in this case is to start by saying, "I didn't want to call you because I don't know what I'm doing, but my boss threatened me with dismissal and I'm behind on my house payments and…" They may take pity on you.

Read the manual. I know that most manuals have a sedative effect, but if you at least browse through the manual, find out what it covers, look for interesting stuff, and generally poke around, you'll learn about the product. It will surprise you how much you'll retain and how fast you'll be able to find things in the manual the next time you need to refer to it.

You should also note all of the useful information in the manual. If you own it, try using Post-It notes to mark the useful pages. (If you share the manual, other people will remove them or add their own until every page is tagged.)

If the operating system you're using has a help system, use it. For example, under Windows, there's a Bookmark facility for tagging useful pages and a Cardfile program for keeping notes on useful information.

Rule 2: Be Organized

When you're trying to get support for a problem, you should have good notes about what has been happening and under what conditions. Have copies of relevant information available when the support people ask for them. This usually requires you to sit in front of the computer—it's almost impossible to guess what they might ask you.

Keep detailed notes of who you spoke to in technical support and when. Occasionally you'll talk to a tech support engineer who really knows how to solve problems. Woe betide you if you can't remember his name the next time you have a problem you suspect he can solve.

Rule 3: Be Patient and Understanding

Being in technical support is a stressful way to earn a living. Imagine taking one call after another, day after day, every one of them with a problem for you to solve. Worse still, every problem is complex, and most of the callers aren't technically oriented.

It follows that if you're nice to the support engineers, you'll get better service. You also need to be understanding, because there will be times when they can't help you. This is sometimes because they simply can't solve the problem, sometimes because the problem has no solution until the next release of the product, and often because the problem isn't in their product but in another vendor's product. This last kind of problem is common in networking, where interactions between hardware and software components are complex.

The System Log

I recommend that all organizations that use computers keep a system log. This is a journal of what hardware and software you have, who installed it, when and where, what configuration was set up, when backups and restores were done, and anything else that's relevant to describing and documenting the system.

If no such log exists or it doesn't cover your PC in depth, consider keeping your own. If you know what hardware and software you have and the details of its setup, often you can solve simple problems on your own. Also, when you need help, the support people won't have to grill you for details or wait while you look for the information they need. For each networked PC, you should know the following:

- ✖ **General hardware:** Which vendors supplied the system components? What type of microprocessor do you have? How much memory do you have, and how fast is it? What type and size is the hard disk? What adapters are installed? What interrupts and input/output addresses are in use by those adapters?

- ✖ **Network hardware:** What kind of network interface card do you have? What build version is it? What options are set (jumpers, switches, and so on)?

NOTE:

When vendors build products, they make minor (or sometimes major) changes in successive batches (or *builds*) to correct problems and faults. Sometimes knowing exactly what build version you have can be a shortcut in resolving why a piece of hardware doesn't work.

✖ **PC operating system:** What version of the operating system is loaded, and what options are installed? What configurations have been selected?

✖ **Memory resident programs:** What terminate-and-stay resident programs (other than networking software) are used? These include device drivers (for tape storage systems, Bernoulli drives, communications cards) and utilities, such as Borland's Sidekick or electronic mail services.

✖ **Configuration data:** A basic MS-DOS system has two configuration files: CONFIG.SYS and AUTOEXEC.BAT. Windows has two additional files: WIN.INI and SYSTEM.INI. Applications under both MS-DOS and Windows often create their own configuration files. If you print the contents of the CONFIG.SYS, AUTOEXEC.BAT, WIN.INI, and SYSTEM.INI files or keep copies of them on a floppy disk, you may save yourself a lot of time when you need to refer to the configuration of a system that isn't running.

✖ **Network cable:** What type of cable is being used? Is the cable that connects your PC to the network the same as other people's?

✖ **Network software:** What version of each network software component is being used? What are the file sizes and creation dates of each component (so if they're somehow damaged you'll know whether the file is intact)? What interrupts are being used? How much memory was available before the network software was loaded, and how much afterward?

NOTE:

File sizes can change due to several types of events. Sometimes disk errors can truncate a file and corrupt it. Other software can cause a wide range of strange problems due to bugs. Computer viruses often make files bigger by adding their code to them. Because of this, you should know not only the file's size and creation date, but also its checksum.

A *checksum* is a value that's derived by combining the values of each character in a file or any other block of data. This is done in a special way that results in a value particular to that data. If even a single character is changed in the data, you'll get a different value when you recalculate the checksum. This makes checksumming a sensitive test for file corruption.

Chasing Problems

Problem chasing begins when you have problems with joining the network or getting a network connection. The following flowcharts depict a generic approach to determining where connection problems lie. You need to trace the connection until you find where the problem goes away. Then work backwards, adding components to the system one by one until you hone in on what's contributing to the problem. This kind of organized, sequential approach is the only way to solve problems.

Some Common Problems

There are many kinds of problems that occur on different networks, but some of them are common to all networks. Many are so glaringly obvious that it's hardly worth listing them, such as running out of disk space or not being able to write to a read-only file. When these kinds of problems occur, only the most pathetic and naively written programs will foul up, but when they do, it's always worth looking for the simple answers first. Figures B.1–B.3 make up a flowchart for tracking down problems.

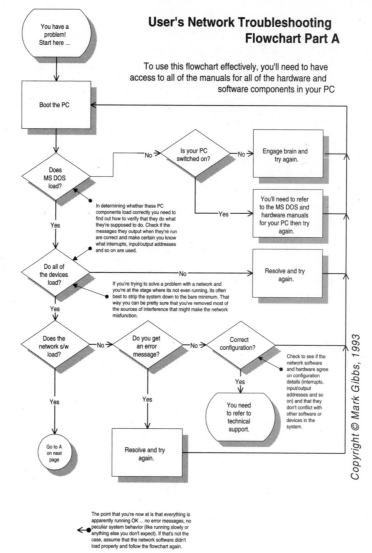

Figure B.1.
A flowchart for tracking down connection problems (Part A).

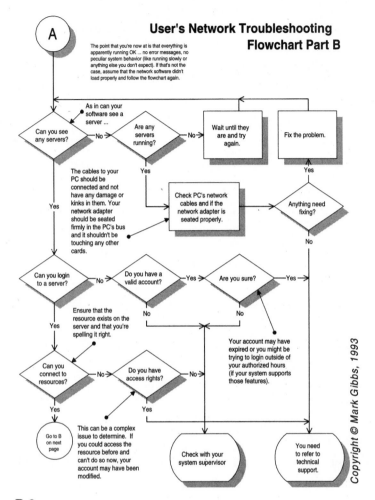

Figure B.2.

Part B of the flowchart for tracking down connection problems.

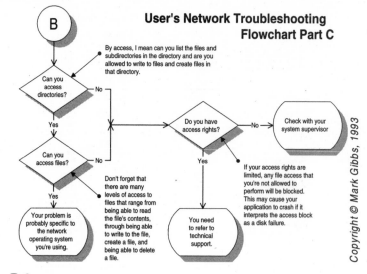

Figure B.3.

Part C of the flowchart for tracking down connection problems.

Unreliable Server Connections

✸ **Problem:** I keep losing my server connections, and there's no pattern to the problem.

Cause: There may be an intermittent fault in either your network interface card or the server's.

Solution: Test the network interface cards and replace if necessary.

✸ **Problem:** It wasn't that. What's next?

Cause: Cable faults may be causing retries that occasionally get so bad that the connection is terminated.

Solution: Repair the cables.

✸ **Problem:** No, the cable is good (or so the supervisor says).

Cause: A PC on the network may be sending invalid messages due to out-of-date network software.

Solution: Check and upgrade all network PC software.

✸ **Problem:** Whenever Bill's PC joins the network, I lose my connection.

Cause: On networks where the PC's address can be set by the installer (ARCnet, for example), two PCs may have the same address.

Solution: Find the PCs with the same address and reconfigure one of them.

NOTE:

You can't (or perhaps I should say *shouldn't*) get two EtherNet network interface cards with the same address. Manufacturers are alloted blocks of EtherNet addresses by the Institute of Electronic and Electrical Engineers (the IEEE, which manages the EtherNet standard), and the convention is that no address will ever be reused. EtherNet addresses are six bytes long, which means more than 70,000,000,000,000 unique addresses are possible, more than enough for the next few centuries. The IEEE charges for this service, which is the neatest way of making money I've ever heard. Imagine the advertising: "Hurry, hurry, hurry. Only 70,000,000 addresses left. Buy yours while they're still available. Double coupons this week…"

Poor Performance

✖ **Problem:** Getting files from the server seems slow.

Cause: The server may be overloaded. As the number of clients increases, performance decreases.

Solution: A more powerful server is needed. (It's only money.)

✖ **Problem:** All servers seem slow, not just one particular server.

Cause: The network may be overloaded or damaged. Each network technology handles increasing loads differently. Some degrade smoothly; others handle the load smoothly until a certain point, after which performance drops catastrophically. If the network cable is damaged, it can corrupt transmissions. Every time a transmission fails it must be retried, so if a section of cable is bad, bandwidth may be wasted on retries.

Solution: If it's an overload, the supervisor needs to subdivide the network, use multiple servers, and possibly use routers to control traffic flow. If this isn't enough, all you can do is wait until the other guys go away and do something else. If the cable is damaged, bug the network supervisor to fix it.

✖ **Problem:** The servers and the network aren't heavily loaded, but performance sucks (as they say in networking circles).

Cause: Another PC may be causing a problem. For example, on a Token Ring network it's possible for a PC to *beacon*—due to a hardware fault, the PC just sends streams of messages and clogs up the network.

Solution: Find the culprit PC and reprogram it with an axe. (Check with the network supervisor first.) The other alternative is to fix the errant machine.

- **Problem:** The performance of my PC is poor, but nobody else is complaining. I'm running out of patience.

  Cause: Assuming that your PC isn't just slow, the network interface card may have developed a fault. There are many hardware faults that can cause this kind of problem. Alternatively, the network adapter cards may just not be fast enough.

  Solution: Test and, if necessary, repair. If it's just slow hardware, it's time to dig into that pocket again.

- **Problem:** I've eliminated all other potential problems and it's still running too slowly!

  Cause: It's possible that the server may not be configured correctly. In many network technologies, various parameters of the server's operation can be configured. The configuration that worked for five clients may be incorrect for 10 clients.

  Solution: The server needs to be reconfigured; send the supervisor e-mail until he gets to it.

Application Problems

- **Problem:** My application can't open files or see what files are in a directory.

  Cause: You may not have sufficient rights in the directories where you're trying to use the application.

  Solution: Get adequate rights, or work in a directory where you have adequate rights.

- **Problem:** The application won't run with the network software loaded.

  Cause: The application probably wasn't installed properly or may be designed not to work on a network. It's also possible that the application just isn't compatible with your network.

  Solution: Install the application correctly for your network. Check the documentation. The vendor may require you to use a different version on a network—they set it up so the application is disabled if it detects a network. Failing that, check with the application vendor to see if they know of any reason why it shouldn't run.

✖ **Problem:** The application can't find data files.

Cause: The files may be in use by another PC, the search drives or paths may not be set up, or the user may not have adequate rights to use the files.

Solution: Make the files sharable (if appropriate), use the right search paths/drives, or get the required rights.

✖ **Problem:** Applications that perform serial input/output lose incoming data.

Cause: This is because access to the network requires computer power; there may not be a lot left for other applications. The result is that serial communications (which are time-sensitive) may be corrupted.

Solution: Reduce the speed of the serial communications. Also, if you're running Windows, or any other operating system or utility under MS-DOS that works in the background, disable it or configure it to run more slowly while you're using the serial port.

Printing Problems

✖ **Problem:** I can't print on a network printer.

Cause: Your PC may not be connected to the network printer.

Solution: Check your network printer connections.

✖ **Problem:** I can print to the network printer, but my job doesn't actually print.

Cause: If other people's jobs are printing but yours are not, you may be sending your jobs to a queue that is either halted or set at a lower priority than the queue other people are using.

Solution: Use the queue they're using, or have an administrator start your queue or raise its priority. (Or if you're senior to the supervisor, insist that the other queue be stopped because your job is the most important.)

✖ **Problem:** My printer output is garbled.

Cause: This can happen if your application isn't configured for the type of printer you're printing on. It can also be caused by various configuration options available with the printing services of many network operating systems. These configuration options reset printers between jobs (to ensure that the printer is ready for the next user's job), convert tabs into spaces, and perform other manipulations of the data. Sometimes these settings cause problems. (For example, if you may accidentally convert what look like tabs to spaces in the middle of graphics data.)

Solution: Check what kind of printer your application thinks it's outputting to, and see whether any of the printer configuration options are set. This might be something to check with your system supervisor.

✖ **Problem:** The printer is sooooooooooooooooo slow.

Cause: The printing system may not be configured correctly. The printing system, under most network operating systems, runs alongside all the other systems that provide services. To optimize performance, many NOSes allow you to select the amount of time allocated for each system to be run. If the printer system's allocation is too small, it may only have time to send a few characters per second from the server to the printer.

Solution: The supervisor needs to reconfigure the printing system.

Summary of Problem Solving

Problem solving is an art. It requires as much intelligence as it does intuition, and as much patience as it does persistence. Some other people's thoughts on this subject:

> "I have yet to see any problem, however complicated, which, looked at the right way, did not become still more complicated."–Paul Anderson

Although it may sometimes seem that Paul Anderson was right, the fact is that the right way he was talking about was, in fact, the wrong way. It's rare that a methodical approach will not find the cause of a problem.

> "The precise statement of any problem is the most important step in its solution."–Edwin Bliss

To be able to precisely define your problem, you need to have access to all of the relevant manuals, know how your PC is configured, and know what it's trying to connect to or work with.

If you think networks are horribly complicated and perhaps more trouble than they're worth, ponder the following thought:

> "If you find a path with no obstacles, it probably doesn't lead anywhere."–Frank A. Clark

Glossary

If you follow the computer business at even the most casual level, you know that it generates terms for new techniques and technologies at an alarming rate. This makes staying up to date a difficult task—just decoding the established stuff can be tough enough. The following glossary is by no means exhaustive, but is intended as a survival guide so that when people say things like, "We've just had a disk crash on one of the duplexed drives in the NetWare file server," you'll be able to respond with, "But we're still online, aren't we?"

10Base2 An IEEE standard for using IEEE 802.3 protocol at 10 megabits over thin EtherNet cable.

10Base5 An IEEE standard for using IEEE 802.3 protocol at 10 megabits over thick EtherNet cable.

10BaseT An IEEE standard for using IEEE 802.3 protocol at 10 megabits over unshielded twisted-pair cable. (The *T* stands for *twisted pair.*)

100BaseVG An IEEE standard for using the new IEEE 802.12 protocol at 100 megabits over unshielded twisted-pair cable of type 5 or type 3. Currently being marketed as AnyLAN by Hewlett Packard, IBM, and others.

100BaseT   A proprietary standard for using IEEE 802.3 protocol at 100 megabits over unshielded twisted-pair cable (at the moment, type 5 cable only). Currently being marketed by a large group of companies, including 3Com, Intel, and others. They are awaiting IEEE standards approval.

802.3   An IEEE standard for the physical layer that specifies a CSMA/CD protocol. This is the standard used for EtherNet.

802.5   An IEEE standard for the physical layer that specifies a token-passing protocol for a ring topology. This is the standard used by Token Ring.

active hub   An ARCnet device used as a cabling center that amplifies and transmits signals to either network nodes or other active or passive hubs. See *hub* and *passive hub*.

AFP   See *AppleTalk File Protocol*.

AnyLAN   See *100BaseVG*.

AppleShare   Apple's file server system.

AppleTalk File Protocol (AFP)   A suite of protocols designed by Apple to support the networking of Macintoshes.

application layer   The uppermost part of the seven-layer OSI reference model. This section contains the user and application programs.

ARCnet (Attached Resource Computing network)   A network transport technology that transfers data using token-passing at 2.5 Mbit/s with coaxial or fiber-optic cable in a modified star topology.

ASCII (American Standard Code for Information Interchange)   A standard that defines which values are used for letters, numbers, and symbols by using a 7-bit code and an 8th check bit.

attenuation   The progressive degradation of a signal as it travels through a cable.

backbone   A network cabling segment that interconnects a group of network segments or systems. The backbone is often dedicated to server traffic or kept between wiring closets (housing MSAUs, concentrators, or hubs) so the systems can operate faster or over longer distances.

back end   A system that provides services for another system. In many cases, the term is synonymous with *server*.

BALUN   A short cable that runs between a workstation and a wall plate, or between MSAUs, concentrators, or hubs. Often this device will make a conversion from one connector type and another. (Sometimes called a *pigtail* or *patch cable*.)

bandwidth   The data-carrying capability of a communications system.

baseband   A communication technique in which network cable is used to carry a single stream of data at a time.

big iron   See *mainframe*.

bridge A device that links two networks that use the same protocol. This may be used to extend the network or to connect two different network transport technologies (such as EtherNet and Token Ring). See *router* and *brouter*.

broadband A communications technique in which network cabling is used to carry multiple streams of data simultaneously.

brouter A device that implements both bridge and router functions. See *bridge* and *router*.

bus A single segment through which items are connected. A PC's expansion bus allows the various components to communicate. A bus network, which is what EtherNet runs on, connects all communicating computers with a common cable.

Carrier Sense Multiple Access with Collision Detection (CSMA/CD) The EtherNet protocol allows each device to create and send its own packets. CSMA/CD is used to avoid excessive collisions between these random launches. A CSMA/CD device first listens for other carriers. If it detects no other carriers, it transmits. If a collision is detected, the device stops transmitting, waits a random length of time, and begins transmitting again. Used in EtherNet and specified by the IEEE standard 802.3.

CCITT Comité Consultatif International Téléphonique et Télégraphique. See *de jure*.

CD-ROM See *compact disc read-only memory*.

client A person making use of a particular system or peripheral through a workstation attached to the network.

client/server A form of database server (client/server database) often implemented with SQL or e-mail engines. This server consists of a central machine (server) that processes an application and provides client machines with finished data. The clients give variables to process to the server through a front-end application. (Examples: Oracle and Microsoft SQL for Windows.) *Client/server* is also used to describe distributed processing. Oddly enough, this is the opposite of the preceding definition. It means that a file server is necessary for a distributed processing network. Clients (users on workstations attached to the server) attach to a file server to recover and store files, but the processing of the data is done at the client machine.

coaxial cable Two-conductor cable used for computer networking, in either a thick or thin form. This cable consists of a center core wire (stranded or single core) covered by insulation, a second conductor of woven wire, and an external covering of plenum (fire-resistant coating) or rubber. Thin coax resembles television cable. Thick coax is thicker and often yellow or orange in color.

compact disc read-only memory (CD-ROM) A method of storage that uses compact discs. CD-ROMs have a vast storage capacity but are read-only, so they're most often used for reference material. CD-ROM drives are now included with many computers.

concentrator (often marketed as an EtherNet Hub) A wiring center used for 10BaseT EtherNet in a back-to-center (home run) cabling scheme. This device acts as concentrating point for the bus topology that's required by EtherNet, although EtherNet outwardly appears to be a star topology.

CSMA/CD See *Carrier Sense Multiple Access/Collision Detection.*

daisy-chain Any network topology that joins computers in a chain. (For example, A to B, B to C, C to D.) There should be a terminator on each end computer that signifies that it's an end of the chain and returns the signal. (Examples: Thin EtherNet, AppleTalk.)

data For the purposes of this book, data in its purest form is made up of characters or code either entered by the user or passed between devices that are part of your computer or network.

database Any collection of a data can be referred to as a database (a phone book is a database, for example). In the computer field, this term has come to mean a file or set of files that stores data in a retrievable format for later recovery or record-keeping.

datagram A message that is sent from one computer to another without guaranteed delivery.

data link layer The second layer of the OSI reference model. This layer puts messages together and manages their flow between computers.

data processing The manipulation of data into the form of usable information, often involving sorting, searching, or calculating raw data.

data switch A switch that allows peripherals to be shared by several PCs on a one-at-a-time basis. (Example: A printer A-B switch that allows two users to share an expensive printer.)

DEC See *Digital Equipment Corporation.*

de facto Meaning "from the fact," these are procedures that become standards because everybody decides they're a good idea. See *de jure.*

de jure Meaning "from the law," these are standards that are ratified by an international body. See *de facto.*

Digital Equipment Corporation (DEC) The second largest computer manufacturer in the world.

disk caching The technique of holding a certain amount of frequently used data in memory so that the user can access it faster than if it came directly from the disk.

disk crash Generically used to describe hard disk failure. An authentic disk crash is when a hard disk fails because the read/write heads carve into the disk platters. The parts literally crash.

disk server   A computer running a special operating system that allows remote PCs to access disk sectors on its hard disk. See *file server*.

downloading   A client-initiated transfer of data from a server to the client's own machine. Also used generically to denote file transfers from one system to another.

downsizing   The process by which many companies look at their operations and find ways to reduce overhead by cutting personnel and equipment costs. Often used to describe the implementation of data processing applications on PCs and PC networks that would previously have been done on mainframes or minicomputers, resulting in lower costs for equipment and staff.

duplexed drives   Two hard disk drives on separate disk controllers whose contents are kept identical for fault tolerance reasons.

EISA   See *Extended Industry Standard Architecture*.

electronic mail   An electronic document-exchange tool used for interpersonal communications that can send and receive text, files, and audio items. A central application is responsible for storing the information, forwarding it to the proper recipient, and possibly tracking that activity. A user interface application enables the user to create, retrieve, and send messages.

electronic messaging   The process of sending and receiving brief messages over a network for immediate use or response.

EtherNet   A network protocol that transfers data at 10 Mbit/s across a linear bus topology.

Extended Industry Standard Architecture (EISA)   A 32-bit PC bus architecture, compatible with the ISA standard.

fiber optics   A technology that uses laser light pulses, sent over thin glass fibers, to deliver data at high speeds (up to several gigabits per second).

file server   A computer running a special operating system that allows authenticated PCs to access files (rather than disk sectors) on a shared portion of its hard disk. See *disk server*.

flow control   A mechanism for ensuring that data isn't sent faster than a recipient PC can receive it.

frame   The way a packet is constructed to be sent across a network. Usually constructed with a beginning and ending notation called a header and footer.

front-end   A user-interface application that's used to access the services of another system. In many cases, this term is synonymous with *client*.

gateway   A device that translates data between two systems that are incompatible or that use different protocols.

groupware   Software that's jointly used by members of a group to work and communicate with each other in a task-specific context. (Examples: shared scheduling, document editing, project planning.)

heterogeneous network   A network operating system that communicates with and can be used by clients that use many different operating systems and methods of file storage and communications. (The opposite is *homogeneous* networking.)

home run   A slang term used by cabling professionals and network administrators for a cabling configuration in which all cables go from nodes on the network back to a center location. (Examples: ARCnet, 10BaseT EtherNet, and IBM Token Ring.)

hub   A cabling center in a star topology that either amplifies a signal and transmits it (active hub) or simply passes the signal along (passive hub). This term is properly used to describe such devices in ARCnet networks, but it has become generic, describing all devices used in a back-to-center (home run) cabling configuration. (Examples: 10BaseT EtherNet concentrators and Token Ring MSAUs, which technically are not hubs.) See *concentrator* and *multistation access unit.*

IBM   See *International Business Machines.*

IEEE   The Institute of Electronic and Electrical Engineers. See *de jure.*

Industry Standard Architecture (ISA)   A 16-bit PC bus architecture

that was originally used in the IBM AT. Also referred to as an AT bus.

information   Data that has been converted into a meaningful form. See *data.* ("Information is data imbued with meaning and purpose."—Prof. P. Drucker.)

information processing   The concept that information, rather than data, is what matters to an organization; this came about with the PC revolution. See *information.*

International Business Machines (IBM)   Originators of the IBM PC and the current Intel-based ISA PCs. It's the largest computer company in the world, manufacturing mainframe and mid-range computers as well as personal computers and operating systems.

Internetwork Packet Exchange (IPX)   The default packet protocol for Novell's NetWare operating system.

interpersonal network (IPN)   See *peer-to-peer network.*

IPX   See *Internetwork Packet Exchange.*

ISA   See *Industry Standard Architecture.*

ISO   International Standards Organization. See *Open Systems Interconnection.*

LAN   See *local area network.*

LANtastic   Artisoft's peer-to-peer network operating system.

local area network (LAN)   A network of computers and peripherals that spans a small physical area, usually one building or a small campus.

LocalTalk   Apple's network transport technology, which transfers data at 256 kilobits per second over a bus network.

logical drive   A non-physical pointer to a specific location on a physical drive or to the physical drive itself. For example, the F: drive could be pointing you to the SYSTEM directory of the SYS: volume on the first physical hard drive in your NetWare server, or it could be pointing you to the CD-ROM drive on your local PC. The pointer is simply a logical presentation created for the user.

login name   The name that a user enters to identify himself to the system.

mainframe   A large central computer whose processing power and peripherals are shared by many people through unintelligent terminals and/or terminal emulation software. Mainframes are physically big and environmentally demanding (just one of them takes up an entire room and requires environmental conditioning), and are designed to process large amounts of data—hence the term *data processing*. See *minicomputers*.

MAN   See *metropolitan area network*.

MCA   See *MicroChannel Architecture*.

metropolitan area network (MAN)   A network that covers a city (tens of miles) and operates at data rates similar to a LAN. Usually owned by service companies that resell the data service to end-users.

MicroChannel Architecture (MCA)   An IBM proprietary 32-bit architecture PC bus architecture that's completely incompatible with all previous hardware designs.

middleware   In a client/server system, software that sits between the client and the server and provides services to facilitate that relationship. See *client/server*.

minicomputer   The successor to the mainframe that offered less computing power for a lot less money and demanded a less controlled environment. See *mainframe*.

mirrored drives   Two hard disk drives attached to the same disk controller, whose contents are kept identical for fault tolerance reasons.

MSAU   See *multistation access unit*.

multistation access unit (MSAU)   The wiring center of a Token Ring network topology, usually consisting of eight node ports, one Ring In port, and one Ring Out port. (These two ports connect the MSAU.)

NDS   See *NetWare Directory Services*.

NETBIOS (Network Basic Input/ Output System)   A standard for supporting network communications that is independent of the underlying network transport type.

NetWare   Novell's Network Operating System (NOS) line.

NetWare Directory Services (NDS)   The distributed directory service for NetWare 4.0.

NetWare Lite   Novell's previous peer-to-peer network operating system. See *Personal NetWare.*

network adapter card   See *network interface card.*

network interface card (NIC)   An expansion card that enables a PC to communicate on a network.

network layer   The third layer of the OSI reference model. This layer is responsible for controlling message traffic.

NFS   A network file system developed by Sun Microsystems for shared files over a UNIX platform. This standard has been adopted by many other vendors.

NIC   See *network interface card.*

node   Another name for a computer or device (such as a printer or modem) that is connected to a network.

noise   Electrical disturbances that corrupt and degrade signals transmitted over cables.

non-dedicated server   A server that can run applications (word processors, spreadsheets, and so on) while it's providing network services to other computers. This is acceptable in a peer-to-peer network environment such as LANtastic or NetWare Lite, but is usually not a good idea in a file server environment such as NetWare 2.x. Most file server environments do not support non-dedicated operation.

NOS   Network operating system.

OEM   See *original equipment manufacturer.*

online   Attached to a network of any kind. This term is often used to describe a service that can be accessed through standard telephone lines.

Open Systems Interconnection (OSI)   A body of standards set by the International Standards Organization to define the activities that must occur when computers communicate. There are seven layers, and each contains a specific set of rules to follow at that point in the communication.

original equipment manufacturer (OEM)   A company that purchases original equipment from the manufacturer and remarkets the product, usually with some value added.

OSI   See *Open Systems Interconnection.*

OSI model   See *Open Systems Interconnection.*

passive hub   An ARCnet device used as a cabling center that passes signals, without amplifying them, to either network nodes or active hubs. See *active hub* and *hub*.

peer-to-peer network   A network system consisting of workstations that are capable of being both server and client.

Personal NetWare   Novell's most recent entry into the peer-to-peer networking scene, offering a more robust and Windows-aware interface.

physical layer   The first layer of the OSI reference model. This layer manages the transfer of individual bits of data over wires or whatever medium is used to connect the communicating computers.

presentation layer   The sixth layer of the OSI reference model. This layer is where the formatting and translation of data is performed so that the application layer can understand what's going on.

proprietary   In the computer industry, this term is often used to imply that a product is owned and controlled by a single vendor.

protocol   A set of rules and procedures that govern the exchange of data between two communicating systems. See *protocol suite*.

protocol suite   When communications between two systems can be for many different purposes, different protocols may exist for those different purposes, all based on a common architecture. These protocols are referred to as a protocol suite. See *protocol*.

record   A collection of data about a particular item. A record is broken up into fields of fixed or variable length that contain specific pieces of data about the general item. Examples of fields include name, address, phone number, etc. All of them together would be a record for a specific person. Many records would make a database.

record locking   Any method of ensuring that a program that accesses a shared database gets exclusive access to a record. See *record*.

recursive   See *recursive*.

redirector   A network software component that gets requests for data and services from a local operating system and sends them to a network server.

remote booting   The technique of downloading from a server to a PC the programs and data required to initialize and execute the PC's operating system and network connection.

repeater   A device that connects network segments, amplifying and regenerating signals for better distance.

ring   A network topology that joins each computer to those on either side, forming a closed circle. See *Token Ring*.

router   A device that links networks that are running different protocols. It can be used to separate unwanted traffic on either side of the bridge, to reduce the traffic, or to provide security from unwanted users. See *brouter* and *bridge*.

439

Sequenced Packet Exchange (SPX) Novell's guaranteed-delivery version of IPX.

session A logical connection between two communicating systems that allows for the transfer of data.

session layer The fifth layer of the OSI reference model. It's responsible for the security and administrative tasks of communicating.

SFT See *System Fault Tolerance.*

shell A software module that intercepts requests for data and services from programs and sends them to a network server if those requests can't be serviced by the local operating system.

SNA See *System Network Architecture.*

SPX See *Sequenced Packet Exchange.*

SQL See *Structured Query Language.*

star A network topology in which all computers communicate through a single, central device.

station See *workstation.*

store-and-forward A technique in which a system accepts data and stores it so that it can be passed (forwarded) to another system at a later time.

StreetTalk The distributed directory service for Banyan VINES. See *VINES.*

Structured Query Language (SQL) A data-sorting language, used as a front-end or client to make requests of a relational database service.

System 7 The operating system for the Macintosh that includes peer-to-peer network services.

System Fault Tolerance (SFT) Both a generic industry term and Novell's name for three levels of service (SFT level I—database translation tracking services; SFT level II—drive mirroring or duplexing; SFT level III—server mirroring) that are offered in file server operating system products. It refers to a system's capability to tolerate and continue though errors.

System Network Architecture (SNA) IBM's architecture for supporting computer communications between dissimilar systems.

terminators Devices that are used at the ends of a linear bus network segment to reflect the signal back and prevent failure of the segment.

thick EtherNet A cabling system for EtherNet connections that uses a heavyweight coaxial cable; this is used for particularly long connections or heavy traffic.

thin EtherNet A cabling system for EtherNet connections that uses a lightweight coaxial cable; this is used for node connections and smaller networks.

token A special message that signifies that the possessor has the right to send messages on a network system.

Token Ring A network transport technology in which a token is passed around in a ring topology, transferring data at either 4 or 16 Mbit/s.

topology The way that a network is physically laid out.

Transaction Tracking System (TTS) Novell's system for ensuring the integrity of a file server's databases by backing out of incomplete file writes and returning to the last complete version.

transport layer The fourth layer of the OSI reference model. This is responsible for error checking, correction, and some message flow control.

TTS See *Transaction Tracking System.*

uploading A client-initiated transfer of data to a server. It's also used generically to denote file transfers from one system to another.

VINES (VIrtual NEtwork System) Banyan's network operating system.

WAN See *wide area network.*

wide area network (WAN) Any network that covers a wide area and requires special communication devices to make connection possible. The largest differences between WANs and LANs are the need to make connections over long distances and the need for telephone, satellite, or microwave equipment to facilitate the connection.

workstation Another name for a computer or device (such as a printer or modem) that is connected to a network. It's also used for the top-end computers, usually UNIX-based, that are used in engineering and graphical environments.

WORM See *write once, read many.*

write once, read many (WORM) A data drive that uses media similar to CD-ROMs. You can write to the disc once and then read from it as many times as you like. Often used for permanent archival of data.

X.400 A standard for electronic messaging defined by the CCITT.

X.500 A protocol standard for global directory services that's currently being developed by the CCITT.

Xerox Network Systems (XNS) Xerox's protocol for network communications.

XNS See *Xerox Network Systems.*

Network Product Vendors

The following list is a small sampling of the thousands of vendors that are active in networking. To find out which vendor sells a particular product, you should read the trade papers and any of the many magazines that cover networking. Another great resource is CompuServe, where you'll find not only vendors but also users who can tell you if the vendors are any good.

3Com Corp
5400 Bayfront Plaza, P.O. Box 58145
Santa Clara, CA 95052-8145
Network infrastructure products
800-638-3266

Accton Technology Corp
46750 Fremont Blvd, Suite 104
Fremont, CA 94538
NIC and network management
800-926-9288

Action Technologies
2200 Powell Street
11th Floor
Emeryville, CA 94608
Telephone: (800) 624-2162

Advanced Computer Communications
720 Santa Barbara Street
Santa Barbara, CA 93101-2299
Bridges, routers, and network management
800-444-7854

Andrew Network Products Corp.
2771 Plaza del Amo
Torrance, CA 90503
Bridges, routers, and NICs
800-733-0331

Apple Computer, Inc.
20525 Mariani Avenue
Cupertino, CA 95014
Macintosh networking products
800-776-2333

Artisoft, Inc.
575 East River Road
Tucson, AZ 85704
Lantastic NOS
800-846-9726

Banyan Systems, Inc.
120 Flanders Road
Westborough, MA 01581
VINES
800-828-2404

Beyond, Inc.
38 Sidney Street
Cambridge, MA 02139
Telephone: (617) 621-0095
Fax: (617) 621-0096

Borland International
1800 Green Falls Road
P.O. Box 660001
Scotts Valley, CA 95067-0001
Telephone: (800) 331-0877/(408) 438-8400
Fax: (408) 439-9272

CBIS
5875 Peachtree Industrial Boulevard
Building 100, Unit 170
Norcross, GA 30092
Telephone: (404) 446-1332

Cheyenne Software, Inc.
55 Bryant Avenue
Roslyn, NY 11576-9850
Telephone: (800) 243-9462/(516) 484-5110
Fax: (516) 484-3446

Coactive Computing Corporation
1301 Shoreway Road
Suite 221
Belmont, CA 94002
Telephone: (415) 802-1080
Fax: (415) 593-9304

Compex
4055 East La Palma Avenue
Suite C
Anaheim, CA 92807
Telephone: (714) 630-7302

Cabletron Systems, Inc.
35 Industrial Way, P.O. Box 5005
Rochester, NH 03867-5005
NICs, bridges, routers, and network management
603-332-9400

Codenoll Technology
1086 North Broadway
Yonkers, NY 10701
EtherNet and FDDI cards and network management software
914-965-6300

DaVinci Systems
P.O. Box 17449
Raleigh, NC 27619
Telephone: (800) 326-3556

Digital Communications Associates, Inc. (DCA)
1000 Alderman Drive
Alpharetta, GA 30202-4199
Telephone: (800) 348-3221/(404) 442-4000
Fax: (404) 442-4366

DSC Communications Corp.
1000 Coit Road
Plano, TX 75075
Telephone: (800) 322-3101/(214) 519-3000

Futurus, Inc.
3131 North I-10 Service Road
Suite 401
Metairie, LA 70002
Telephone: (800) 327-8296/(504) 837-1554
Fax: (504) 837-3429

Grapevine LAN Products
15323 Northeast 90th Street
Redmond, WA 98052
Telephone: (206) 869-2707

David Harris
Pegasus Mail
P.O. Box 5451
Dunedin, New Zealand

Hayes Microcomputer Products
P.O. Box 105203
Atlanta, GA 30348
Telephone: (404) 441-1617

International Business Machines Corporation (IBM)
(check for a local office or call Enquiries at 800-426-3333)
LAN Server NOS

Invisible Software
1165 Chess Drive
Suite D
Foster City, CA 94404
Telephone: (415) 570-5967

LanMark
P.O. Box 246
Postal Station A
Mississauga, ON, Canada L5A 3G8
Telephone: (416) 848-6865

Lotus Development Corporation
55 Cambridge Parkway
Cambridge, MA 02142
Telephone: (617) 577-8500
Fax: (617) 693-4663

Microsoft Corporation
One Microsoft Way
Redmond, WA 98052
Windows NT Advanced Server NOS and Windows for Workgroups
206-936-2655

Notework Corporation
72 Kent Street
Brookline, MA 02146
Telephone: (617) 734-4317

NetFrame Systems, Inc.
1545 Barber Lane
Milpitas, CA 95035
Super-servers
800-852-3726

Novell
122 E 1700 S
Provo, UT 84606
NetWare, WordPerfect, TCP/IP products
800-453-1267

Performance Technology
7800 IH 10, West
800 Lincoln Center
San Antonio, TX 78230
Telephone: (800) 327-8526/(512) 524-0500 or 2000

PowerCore, Inc.
1 Diversatech Drive
Manteno, IL 60950
Telephone: (800) 237-4754/(815) 468-3737
Fax: (815) 468-3867

Sitka Corporation
950 Marina Village Parkway
Alameda, CA 94501
Telephone: (800) 445-8677/(415) 769-9669
Fax: (415) 769-8771

Thomas-Conrad Corporation
1908-R Kramer Lane
Austin, TX 78758
Telephone: (800) 332-8683/(512) 836-1935
Fax: (512) 836-2840

WordPerfect Corporation
1555 North Technology Way
Orem, UT 84057
Telephone: (800) 321-4566

Product Directory

Product Name	Vendor
Peer-to-Peer Systems	
10NetPlus	Digital Communications Associates, Sitka
Coactive Connector	Coactive Computing
EasyNet	LanMark
GV LAN OS	Grapevine LAN Products
LANsmart	D-Link Systems
LANsoft	ACCTON Technology
LANStep	Hayes Microcomputer Products
LANtastic	Artisoft
Macintosh System 7	Apple Computer
NET/30	Invisible Software
NetWare Lite	Novell
Network OS	CBIS
POWERLan	Performance Technology
ReadyLink	Complex
WEB	WebCorp
Windows for Workgroups	Microsoft
File Server Systems	
LAN Manager	Microsoft
LAN Server	IBM
NetWare	Novell, IBM
VINES	Banyan
Electronic Messaging Products	
BeyondMail	Beyond
cc:Mail	Lotus Development
DaVinci eMAIL	DaVinci Systems
MAPI	Microsoft

Product Name	Vendor
Electronic Messaging Products	
MHS	Novell
Microsoft Mail	Microsoft
Noteworks	Notework
Pegasus Mail	David Harris
VIM	Lotus Development
WordPerfect Office	WordPerfect
Groupware	
Futurus Team	Futurus
Network Scheduler	PowerCore
Notes	Lotus Development Corporation
Schedule+	Microsoft
The Coordinator	DaVinci Systems

Index

Q-R

Add to Your Sams Library Today with the Best Books for Programming, Operating Systems, and New Technologies

The easiest way to order is to pick up the phone and call

1-800-428-5331

between 9:00 a.m. and 5:00 p.m. EST.
For faster service please have your credit card available.

ISBN	Quantity	Description of Item	Unit Cost	Total Cost
0-672-30510-0		Absolute Beginner's Guide to C, 2nd Edition	$22.00	
0-672-30460-0		Absolute Beginner's Guide to UNIX	$19.99	
0-672-30269-1		Absolute Beginner's Guide to Programming	$19.95	
0-672-30342-6		Absolute Beginner's Guide to QBasic	$16.95	
0-672-30501-1		Understanding Data Communications, 4th Edition	$29.99	
0-672-30362-0		Navigating the Internet	$24.95	
0-672-30466-X		The Internet Unleashed (Book/Disk)	$39.95	
0-672-30440-6		Database Developer's Guide with Visual Basic 3.0	$44.95	
0-672-30384-1		Word for Windows 6.0 Super Book (Book/Disk)	$39.95	
0-672-30413-9		Multimedia Madness!, Deluxe Edition (Book/Disk/CD-ROM)	$55.00	
0-672-30450-3		Edutainment Comes Alive!	$39.99	
❏ 3 ½" Disk		Shipping and Handling: See information below.		
❏ 5 ¼" Disk		TOTAL		

Shipping and Handling: $4.00 for the first book, and $1.75 for each additional book. Floppy disk: add $1.75 for shipping and handling. If you need to have it NOW, we can ship product to you in 24 hours for an additional charge of approximately $18.00, and you will receive your item overnight or in two days. Overseas shipping and handling adds $2.00 per book and $8.00 for up to three disks. Prices subject to change. Call for availability and pricing information on latest editions.

201 W. 103rd Street, Indianapolis, Indiana 46290

1-800-428-5331 — Orders   1-800-835-3202 — FAX   1-800-858-7674 — Customer Service

Book ISBN 0-672-30553-4